THIS BOOK
BELONGS TO

_____

_____

PLATE I
Bellerophon on Pegasus

Greek Myths

A Wonder Book for Girls and Boys

Nathaniel Hawthorne
Illustrated by Walter Crane

BARNES & NOBLE
NEW YORK

This 2012 edition published by Barnes & Noble, Inc.

Cover art: Kate Forrester
Cover design: Jo Obarowski
Book design: Patrice Kaplan

Barnes & Noble, Inc.
122 Fifth Avenue
New York, NY 10011

ISBN: 978-1-4351-4283-1

Printed and bound in China

1 3 5 7 9 10 8 6 4 2

CONTENTS

THE THREE GOLDEN APPLES

THE MIRACULOUS PITCHER

THE CHIMÆRA

LIST OF PLATES

LIST OF DESIGNS

THE AUTHOR HAS LONG BEEN OF OPINION THAT MANY OF THE classical myths were capable of being rendered into very capital reading for children. In the little volume here offered to the public, he has worked up half a dozen of them, with this end in view. A great freedom of treatment was necessary to his plan; but it will be observed by every one who attempts to render these legends malleable in his intellectual furnace, that they are marvelously independent of all temporary modes and circumstances. They remain essentially the same, after changes that would affect the identity of almost anything else.

He does not, therefore, plead guilty to a sacrilege, in having sometimes shaped anew, as his fancy dictated, the forms that have been hallowed by an antiquity of two or three thousand years. No epoch of time can claim a copyright in these immortal fables. They seem never to have been made; and certainly, so long as man exists, they can never perish; but, by their indestructibility itself, they are legitimate subjects for every age to clothe with its own garniture of manners and sentiment, and to imbue with its own morality. In the present version they may have lost much of their classical aspect (or, at all events, the author has not been careful to preserve it), and have perhaps assumed a Gothic or romantic guise.

In performing this pleasant task,—for it has been really a task fit for hot weather, and one of the most agreeable, of a literary kind, which he ever undertook,—the author has not always thought it necessary to write downward, in order to meet the comprehension of children. He has generally suffered the theme to soar, whenever such was its tendency, and when he himself was buoyant enough to follow without an effort. Children possess an unestimated sensibility to whatever is deep or high, in imagination or feeling, so long as it is simple, likewise. It is only the artificial and the complex that bewilder them.

LENOX, *July* 15, 1851.

INTRODUCTORY TO
THE GORGON'S HEAD

ENEATH THE PORCH OF THE COUNTRY-seat called Tanglewood, one fine autumnal morning, was assembled a merry party of little folks, with a tall youth in the midst of them. They had planned a nutting expedition, and were impatiently waiting for the mists to roll up the hill-slopes, and for the sun to pour the warmth of the Indian summer over the fields and pastures, and into the nooks of the many-colored woods. There was a prospect of as fine a day as ever gladdened the aspect of this beautiful and comfortable world. As yet, however, the morning mist filled up the whole length and breadth of the valley, above which, on a gently sloping eminence, the mansion stood.

This body of white vapor extended to within less than a hundred yards of the house. It completely hid everything beyond that distance, except a few ruddy or yellow tree-tops, which here and there emerged, and were glorified by the early sunshine, as was likewise the broad surface of the mist. Four or five miles off to the southward rose the summit of Monument Mountain, and seemed to be floating on a cloud. Some fifteen miles farther away, in the same direction, appeared the loftier Dome of Taconic, looking blue and indistinct, and hardly so substantial as the vapory sea that almost rolled over it. The nearer hills, which bordered the valley, were half submerged, and were specked with little cloud-wreaths all the way to their tops. On the whole, there was so much cloud, and so little solid earth, that it had the effect of a vision.

The children above-mentioned, being as full of life as they could hold, kept overflowing from the porch of Tanglewood, and scampering along the gravel-walk, or rushing across the dewy herbage of the lawn. I can hardly tell how many of these small people there were; not less than nine or ten, however, nor more than a dozen, of all sorts, sizes, and ages, whether girls or boys. They were brothers, sisters, and cousins, together with a few of their young acquaintances, who had been invited by Mr. and Mrs. Pringle to spend some of this delightful weather with their own children at Tanglewood. I am afraid to tell you their names, or even to give them any names which other children have ever been called by; because, to my certain knowledge, authors some-times get themselves into great trouble by accidentally giving the names of real persons to the characters in their books. For this reason I mean to call them Primrose, Periwinkle, Sweet Fern, Dandelion, Blue Eye, Clover, Huckleberry, Cowslip, Squash-Blossom, Milkweed, Plantain, and Buttercup; although, to be sure, such titles might better suit a group of fairies than a com-pany of earthly children.

It is not to be supposed that these little folks were to be permitted by their careful fathers and mothers, uncles, aunts, or grandparents, to stray abroad into the woods and fields, without the guardianship of some particularly grave and elderly person. Oh, no, indeed! In the first sentence of my book, you will recollect that I spoke of a tall youth, standing in the midst of the children. His name—(and I shall let you know his real name, because he considers it a great honor to have told the stories that are here to be printed)—his name was Eustace Bright. He was a student at Williams College, and had reached, I think, at this period, the venerable age of eighteen years; so that he felt quite like a grandfather towards Periwinkle, Dandelion, Huckleberry, Squash-Blossom, Milkweed, and the rest, who were only half or a third as venerable as he. A trouble in his eyesight (such as many students think it necessary to have, nowadays, in order to prove their diligence at their books) had kept him from college a week or two after the beginning of the term. But, for my part, I have seldom met with a pair of eyes that looked as if they could see farther or better than those of Eustace Bright.

This learned student was slender, and rather pale, as all Yankee students are; but yet of a healthy aspect, and as light and active as if he had wings to his shoes. By the by, being much addicted to wading through streamlets and across meadows, he had put on cowhide boots for the expedition. He wore a linen blouse, a cloth cap, and a pair of green spectacles, which he had assumed, probably, less for the preservation of his eyes than for the dignity that they imparted to his countenance. In either case, however, he might as well have let them alone; for Huckleberry, a mischievous little elf, crept behind Eustace as he sat on the steps of the porch, snatched the spectacles from his nose, and clapped them on her own; and as the student forgot to take them back, they fell off into the grass, and lay there till the next spring.

Now, Eustace Bright, you must know, had won great fame among the children, as a narrator of wonderful stories; and though he sometimes pretended to be annoyed, when they teased him for more, and more, and always for more, yet I really doubt whether he liked anything quite so well as to tell them. You might have seen his eyes twinkle, therefore, when Clover, Sweet Fern, Cowslip, Buttercup, and most of their playmates, besought him to relate one of his stories, while they were waiting for the mist to clear up.

"Yes, Cousin Eustace," said Primrose, who was a bright girl of twelve, with laughing eyes, and a nose that turned up a little, "the morning is certainly the best time for the stories with which you so often tire out our patience. We shall be in less danger of hurting your feelings, by falling asleep at the most interesting points,—as little Cowslip and I did last night!"

"Naughty Primrose," cried Cowslip, a child of six years old; "I did not fall asleep, and I only shut my eyes, so as to see a picture of what Cousin Eustace was telling about. His stories are good to hear at night, because we can dream about them asleep; and good in the morning, too, because then we can dream about them awake. So I hope he will tell us one this very minute."

"Thank you, my little Cowslip," said Eustace; "certainly you shall have the best story I can think of, if it were only for defending me so well from that naughty Primrose. But, children, I have already told you so many fairy tales, that I doubt whether there is a single one which you have not heard at least twice over. I am afraid you will fall asleep in reality, if I repeat any of them again."

"No, no, no!" cried Blue Eye, Periwinkle, Plantain, and half a dozen others. "We like a story all the better for having heard it two or three times before."

And it is a truth, as regards children, that a story seems often to deepen its mark in their interest, not merely by two or three, but by numberless repetitions. But Eustace Bright, in the exuberance of his resources, scorned to avail himself of an advantage which an older story-teller would have been glad to grasp at.

"It would be a great pity," said he, "if a man of my learning (to say nothing of original fancy) could not find a new story every day, year in and year out, for children such as you. I will tell you one of the nursery tales that were made for the amusement of our great old grandmother, the Earth, when she was a child in frock and pinafore. There are a hundred such; and it is a wonder to me that they have not long ago been put into picture-books for little girls and boys. But, instead of that, old gray-bearded grandsires pore over them in musty volumes of Greek, and puzzle themselves with trying to find out when, and how, and for what they were made."

"Well, well, well, well, Cousin Eustace!" cried all the children at once; "talk no more about your stories, but begin."

"Sit down, then, every soul of you," said Eustace Bright, "and be all as still as so many mice. At the slightest interruption, whether from great, naughty Primrose, little Dandelion, or any other, I shall bite the story short off between my teeth, and swallow the untold part. But, in the first place, do any of you know what a Gorgon is?"

"I do," said Primrose.

"Then hold your tongue!" rejoined Eustace, who had rather she would have known nothing about the matter. "Hold all your tongues, and I shall tell you a sweet pretty story of a Gorgon's head."

And so he did, as you may begin to read on the next page. Working up his sophomorical erudition with a good deal of tact, and incurring great obligations to Professor Anthon, he, nevertheless, disregarded all classical authorities, whenever the vagrant audacity of his imagination impelled him to do so.

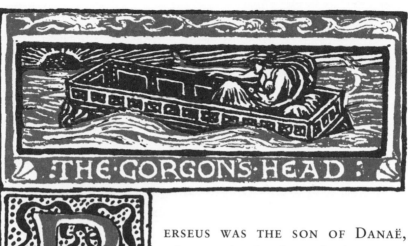

THE·GORGON'S·HEAD·

PERSEUS WAS THE SON OF DANAË, who was the daughter of a king. And when Perseus was a very little boy, some wicked people put his mother and himself into a chest, and set them afloat upon the sea. The wind blew freshly, and drove the chest away from the shore, and the uneasy billows tossed it up and down; while Danaë clasped her child closely to her bosom, and dreaded that some big wave would dash its foamy crest over them both. The chest sailed on, however, and neither sank nor was upset; until, when night was coming, it floated so near an island that it got entangled in a fisherman's nets, and was drawn out high and dry upon the sand. The island was called Seriphus, and it was reigned over by King Polydectes, who happened to be the fisherman's brother.

This fisherman, I am glad to tell you, was an exceedingly humane and upright man. He showed great kindness to Danaë and her little boy; and continued to befriend them, until Perseus had grown to be a handsome youth, very strong and active, and skillful in the use of arms. Long before this time, King Polydectes had seen the two strangers—the mother and her child—who had come to his dominions in a floating chest. As he was not good and kind, like his brother the fisherman, but extremely wicked, he resolved to send Perseus on a dangerous enterprise, in which he would probably be killed, and then to do some great mischief to Danaë herself. So this bad-hearted king spent a long while in considering what was the most dangerous thing that a young man could possibly undertake to perform. At last, having hit upon an enterprise that promised to turn out as fatally as he desired, he sent for the youthful Perseus.

The young man came to the palace, and found the king sitting upon his throne.

"Perseus," said King Polydectes, smiling craftily upon him, "you are grown up a fine young man. You and your good mother have received a great deal of kindness from myself, as well as from my worthy brother the fisherman, and I suppose you would not be sorry to repay some of it."

"Please your Majesty," answered Perseus, "I would willingly risk my life to do so."

"Well, then," continued the king, still with a cunning smile on his lips, "I have a little adventure to propose to you; and, as you are a brave and enterprising youth, you will doubtless look upon it as a great piece of good luck to have so rare an opportunity of distinguishing yourself. You must know, my good Perseus, I think of getting married to the beautiful Princess Hippodamia; and it is customary, on these occasions, to make the bride a present of some far-fetched and elegant curiosity. I have been a little per-plexed, I must honestly confess, where to obtain anything likely to please a princess of her exquisite taste. But, this morning, I flatter myself, I have thought of precisely the article."

"And can I assist your Majesty in obtaining it?" cried Perseus, eagerly.

"You can, if you are as brave a youth as I believe you to be," replied King Polydectes, with the utmost graciousness of manner. "The bridal gift which I have set my heart on presenting to the beautiful Hippodamia is the head of the Gorgon Medusa with the snaky locks; and I depend on you, my dear Perseus, to bring it to me. So, as I am anxious to settle affairs with the princess, the sooner you go in quest of the Gorgon, the better I shall be pleased."

"I will set out to-morrow morning," answered Perseus.

"Pray do so, my gallant youth," rejoined the king. "And, Perseus, in cutting off the Gorgon's head, be careful to make a clean stroke, so as not to injure its appearance. You must bring it home in the very best condition, in order to suit the exquisite taste of the beautiful Princess Hippodamia."

Perseus left the palace, but was scarcely out of hearing before Polydectes burst into a laugh; being greatly amused, wicked king that he was, to find how readily the young man fell into the snare. The news quickly spread abroad that Perseus had undertaken to cut off the head of Medusa with the snaky locks. Everybody was rejoiced; for most of the inhabitants of the island were as wicked as the king himself, and would have liked nothing better than to see some enormous mischief happen to Danaë and her son. The only good man in this unfortunate island of Seriphus appears to have been the fisherman. As Perseus walked along, therefore, the people pointed after him, and made mouths, and winked to one another, and ridiculed him as loudly as they dared.

"Ho, ho!" cried they; "Medusa's snakes will sting him soundly!"

Now, there were three Gorgons alive at that period; and they were the most strange and terrible monsters that had ever been since the world was made, or that have been seen in after days, or that are likely to be seen in all time to come. I hardly know what sort of creature or hobgoblin to call them. They were three sisters, and seem to have borne some distant resemblance to women, but were really a very frightful and mischievous species of dragon. It is, indeed, difficult to imagine what hideous beings these three sisters were. Why, instead of locks of hair, if you can believe me, they had each of them a hundred enormous snakes growing on their heads, all alive, twisting, wriggling, curling, and thrusting out their venomous tongues, with forked stings at the end! The teeth of the Gorgons were terribly long tusks; their hands were made of brass; and their bodies were all over scales, which, if not iron, were something as hard and impenetrable. They had wings, too, and exceedingly splendid ones, I can assure you; for every feather in them was pure, bright, glittering, burnished gold, and they looked very dazzlingly, no doubt, when the Gorgons were flying about in the sunshine.

But when people happened to catch a glimpse of their glittering brightness, aloft in the air, they seldom stopped to gaze, but ran and hid themselves as speedily as they could. You will think, perhaps, that they were afraid of being stung by the serpents that served the Gorgons instead of hair,—or of having their heads bitten off by their ugly tusks,—or of being torn all to pieces by their brazen claws. Well, to be sure, these were some of the dangers, but by no means the greatest, nor the most difficult to avoid. For the worst thing about these abominable Gorgons was, that, if once a poor mortal fixed his eyes full upon one of their faces, he was certain, that very instant, to be changed from warm flesh and blood into cold and lifeless stone!

Thus, as you will easily perceive, it was a very dangerous adventure that the wicked King Polydectes had contrived for this innocent young man. Perseus himself, when he had thought over the matter, could not help seeing that he had very little chance of coming safely through it, and that he was far more likely to become a stone image than to bring back the head of Medusa with the snaky locks. For, not to speak of other difficulties, there was one which it would have puzzled an older man than Perseus to get over. Not only must he fight with and slay this golden-winged, iron-scaled, long-tusked, brazen-clawed, snaky-haired monster, but he must do it with his eyes shut, or, at least, without so much as a glance at the enemy with whom he was contending. Else, while his arm was lifted to strike, he would stiffen into stone, and stand with that uplifted arm for centuries, until time, and the wind and weather, should crumble him quite away. This would be a very sad thing to befall a young man who wanted to perform a great many brave deeds, and to enjoy a great deal of happiness, in this bright and beautiful world.

So disconsolate did these thoughts make him, that Perseus could not bear to tell his mother what he had undertaken to do. He therefore took his shield, girded on his sword, and crossed over from the island to the mainland, where he sat down in a solitary place, and hardly refrained from shedding tears.

NATHANIEL HAWTHORNE

But, while he was in this sorrowful mood, he heard a voice close beside him.

"Perseus," said the voice, "why are you sad?"

He lifted his head from his hands, in which he had hidden it, and, behold! all alone as Perseus had supposed himself to be, there was a stranger in the solitary place. It was a brisk, intelligent, and remarkably shrewd-looking young man, with a cloak over his shoulders, an odd sort of cap on his head, a strangely twisted staff in his hand, and a short and very crooked sword hanging by his side. He was exceedingly light and active in his figure, like a person much accustomed to gymnastic exercises, and well able to leap or run. Above all, the stranger had such a cheerful, knowing, and helpful aspect (though it was certainly a little mischievous, into the bargain), that Perseus could not help feeling his spirits grow livelier as he gazed at him. Besides, being really a courageous youth, he felt greatly ashamed that anybody should have found him with tears in his eyes, like a timid little schoolboy, when, after all, there might be no occasion for despair. So Perseus wiped his eyes, and answered the stranger pretty briskly, putting on as brave a look as he could.

"I am not so very sad," said he, "only thoughtful about an adventure that I have undertaken."

"Oho!" answered the stranger. "Well, tell me all about it, and possibly I may be of service to you. I have helped a good many young men through adventures that looked difficult enough beforehand. Perhaps you may have heard of me. I have more names than one; but the name of Quicksilver suits me as well as any other. Tell me what the trouble is, and we will talk the matter over, and see what can be done."

The stranger's words and manner put Perseus into quite a different mood from his former one. He resolved to tell Quicksilver all his difficulties, since he could not easily be worse off than he already was, and, very possibly, his new friend might give him some advice that would turn out well in the end. So he let the stranger know, in few words, precisely what the case was,—how that King Polydectes wanted the head of Medusa with the snaky locks as a bridal gift for the beautiful Princess Hippodamia, and how that he had undertaken to get it for him, but was afraid of being turned into stone.

"And that would be a great pity," said Quicksilver, with his mischievous smile. "You would make a very handsome marble statue, it is true, and it would be a considerable number of centuries before you crumbled away; but, on the whole, one would rather be a young man for a few years than a stone image for a great many."

"Oh, far rather!" exclaimed Perseus, with the tears again standing in his eyes. "And, besides, what would my dear mother do, if her beloved son were turned into a stone?"

"Well, well, let us hope that the affair will not turn out so very badly," replied Quicksilver, in an encouraging tone. "I am the very person to help you, if anybody can. My sister and myself will do our utmost to bring you safe through the adventure, ugly as it now looks."

"Your sister?" repeated Perseus.

"Yes, my sister," said the stranger. "She is very wise, I promise you; and as for myself, I generally have all my wits about me, such as they are. If you show yourself bold and cautious, and follow our advice, you need not fear being a stone image yet awhile. But, first of all, you must polish your shield, till you can see your face in it as distinctly as in a mirror."

This seemed to Perseus rather an odd beginning of the adventure; for he thought it of far more consequence that the shield should be strong enough to defend him from the Gorgon's brazen claws, than that it should be bright enough to show him the reflection of his face. However, concluding that Quicksilver knew better than himself, he immediately set to work, and scrubbed the shield with so much diligence and good-will, that it very quickly shone like the moon at harvest-time. Quicksilver looked at it with a smile, and nodded his approbation. Then, taking off his own short and crooked sword, he girded it about Perseus, instead of the one which he had before worn.

"No sword but mine will answer your purpose," observed he; "the blade has a most excellent temper, and will cut through iron and brass as easily as through the slenderest twig. And now we will set out. The next thing is to find the Three Gray Women, who will tell us where to find the Nymphs."

"The Three Gray Women!" cried Perseus, to whom this seemed only a new difficulty in the path of his adventure; "pray who may the Three Gray Women be? I never heard of them before."

"They are three very strange old ladies," said Quicksilver, laughing. "They have but one eye among them, and only one tooth. Moreover, you must find them out by starlight, or in the dusk of the evening; for they never show themselves by the light either of the sun or moon."

"But," said Perseus, "why should I waste my time with these Three Gray Women? Would it not be better to set out at once in search of the terrible Gorgons?"

"No, no," answered his friend. "There are other things to be done, before you can find your way to the Gorgons. There is nothing for it but to hunt up these old ladies; and when we meet with them, you may be sure that the Gorgons are not a great way off. Come, let us be stirring!"

Perseus, by this time, felt so much confidence in his companion's sagacity, that he made no more objections, and professed himself ready to begin the adventure immediately. They accordingly set out, and walked at a pretty brisk pace; so brisk, indeed, that Perseus found it rather difficult to keep up with his nimble friend Quicksilver. To say the truth, he had a singular idea that Quicksilver was furnished with a pair of winged shoes, which, of course, helped him along marvelously. And then, too, when Perseus looked sideways at him, out of the corner of his eye, he seemed to see wings on the side of his head; although if he turned a full gaze, there were no such things to be perceived, but only an odd kind of cap. But, at all events, the twisted staff was evidently a great convenience to Quicksilver, and enabled him to proceed so fast, that Perseus, though a remarkably active young man, began to be out of breath.

"Here!" cried Quicksilver, at last,—for he knew well enough, rogue that he was, how hard Perseus found it to keep pace with him,—"take you the staff, for you need it a great deal more than I. Are there no better walkers than yourself in the island of Seriphus?"

"I could walk pretty well," said Perseus, glancing slyly at his companion's feet, "if I had only a pair of winged shoes."

"We must see about getting you a pair," answered Quicksilver.

But the staff helped Perseus along so bravely that he no longer felt the slightest weariness. In fact, the stick seemed to be alive in his hand, and to lend some of its life to Perseus. He and Quicksilver now walked onward at their ease, talking very sociably together; and Quicksilver told so many pleasant stories about his former adventures, and how well his wits had served him on various occasions, that Perseus began to think him a very wonderful person. He evidently knew the world; and nobody is so charming to a young man as a friend who has that kind of knowledge. Perseus listened the more eagerly, in the hope of brightening his own wits by what he heard.

At last, he happened to recollect that Quicksilver had spoken of a sister, who was to lend her assistance in the adventure which they were now bound upon.

"Where is she?" he inquired. "Shall we not meet her soon?"

"All at the proper time," said his companion. "But this sister of mine, you must understand, is quite a different sort of character from myself. She is very grave and prudent, seldom smiles, never laughs, and makes it a rule not to utter a word unless she has something particularly profound to say. Neither will she listen to any but the wisest conversation."

"Dear me!" ejaculated Perseus; "I shall be afraid to say a syllable."

"She is a very accomplished person, I assure you," continued Quicksilver, "and has all the arts and sciences at her fingers' ends. In short, she is so immoderately wise that many people call her wisdom personified. But, to tell you the truth, she has hardly vivacity enough for my taste; and I think you would scarcely find her so pleasant a traveling companion as myself. She has her good points, nevertheless; and you will find the benefit of them, in your encounter with the Gorgons."

By this time it had grown quite dusk. They were now come to a very wild and desert place, overgrown with shaggy bushes, and so silent and solitary that nobody seemed ever to have dwelt or journeyed there. All was waste and desolate, in the gray twilight, which grew every moment more obscure. Perseus looked about him, rather disconsolately, and asked Quicksilver whether they had a great deal farther to go.

"Hist! hist!" whispered his companion. "Make no noise! This is just the time and place to meet the Three Gray Women. Be careful that they do not see you before you see them; for, though they have but a single eye among the three, it is as sharp-sighted as half a dozen common eyes."

"But what must I do," asked Perseus, "when we meet them?"

Quicksilver explained to Perseus how the Three Gray Women managed with their one eye. They were in the habit, it seems, of changing it from one to another, as if it had been a pair of spectacles, or—which would have suited them better—a quizzing-glass. When one of the three had kept the eye a certain time, she took it out of the socket and passed it to one of her sisters, whose turn it might happen to be, and who immediately clapped it into her own head, and enjoyed a peep at the visible world. Thus it will easily be understood that only one of the Three Gray Women could see, while the other two were in utter darkness; and, moreover, at the instant when the eye was passing from hand to hand, neither of the poor old ladies was able to see a wink. I have heard of a great many strange things, in my day, and have witnessed not a few; but none, it seems to me, that can compare with the oddity of these Three Gray Women, all peeping through a single eye.

So thought Perseus, likewise, and was so astonished that he almost fancied his companion was joking with him, and that there were no such old women in the world.

"You will soon find whether I tell the truth or no," observed Quicksilver. "Hark! hush! hist! hist! There they come, now!"

Perseus looked earnestly through the dusk of the evening, and there, sure enough, at no great distance off, he descried the Three Gray Women. The light being so faint, he could not well make out what sort of figures they were; only he discovered that they had long gray hair; and, as they came nearer, he saw that two of them had but the empty socket of an eye, in the middle of their foreheads. But, in the middle of the third sister's forehead, there was a very large, bright, and piercing eye, which sparkled like a great diamond in a ring; and so penetrating did it seem to be, that Perseus could not help thinking it must possess the gift of seeing in the darkest midnight just as perfectly as at noonday. The sight of three persons' eyes was melted and collected into that single one.

Thus the three old dames got along about as comfortably, upon the whole, as if they could all see at once. She who chanced to have the eye in her forehead led the other two by the hands, peeping sharply about her, all the while; insomuch that Perseus dreaded lest she should see right through the thick clump of bushes behind which he and Quicksilver had hidden themselves. My stars! it was positively terrible to be within reach of so very sharp an eye!

But, before they reached the clump of bushes, one of the Three Gray Women spoke.

"Sister! Sister Scarecrow!" cried she, "you have had the eye long enough. It is my turn now!"

"Let me keep it a moment longer, Sister Nightmare," answered Scarecrow. "I thought I had a glimpse of something behind that thick bush."

"Well, and what of that?" retorted Nightmare, peevishly. "Can't I see into a thick bush as easily as yourself? The eye is mine as well as yours; and I know the use of it as well as you, or may be a little better. I insist upon taking a peep immediately!"

But here the third sister, whose name was Shakejoint, began to complain, and said that it was her turn to have the eye, and that Scarecrow and Nightmare wanted to keep it all to themselves. To end the dispute, old Dame Scarecrow took the eye out of her forehead, and held it forth in her hand.

"Take it, one of you," cried she, "and quit this foolish quarreling. For my part, I shall be glad of a little thick darkness. Take it quickly, however, or I must clap it into my own head again!"

Accordingly, both Nightmare and Shakejoint put out their hands, groping eagerly to snatch the eye out of the hand of Scarecrow. But, being both alike blind, they could not easily find where Scarecrow's hand was; and Scarecrow, being now just as much in the dark as Shakejoint and Nightmare, could not at once meet either of their hands, in order to put the eye into it. Thus (as you will see, with half an eye, my wise little auditors), these good old dames had fallen into a strange perplexity. For, though the eye shone and glistened like a star, as Scarecrow held it out, yet the Gray Women caught not the least glimpse of its light, and were all three in utter darkness, from too impatient a desire to see.

Quicksilver was so much tickled at beholding Shakejoint and Nightmare both groping for the eye, and each finding fault with Scarecrow and one another, that he could scarcely help laughing aloud.

"Now is your time!" he whispered to Perseus. "Quick, quick! before they can clap the eye into either of their heads. Rush out upon the old ladies, and snatch it from Scarecrow's hand!"

In an instant, while the Three Gray Women were still scolding each other, Perseus leaped from behind the clump of bushes, and made himself master of the prize. The marvelous eye, as he held it in his hand, shone very brightly, and seemed to look up into his face with a knowing air, and an expression as if it would have winked, had it been provided with a pair of eyelids for that purpose. But the Gray Women knew nothing of what had happened; and, each supposing that one of her sisters was in possession of the eye, they began their quarrel anew. At last, as Perseus did not wish to put these respectable dames to greater inconvenience than was really necessary, he thought it right to explain the matter.

"My good ladies," said he, "pray do not be angry with one another. If anybody is in fault, it is myself; for I have the honor to hold your very brilliant and excellent eye in my own hand!"

"You! you have our eye! And who are you?" screamed the Three Gray Women, all in a breath; for they were terribly frightened, of course, at hearing a strange voice, and discovering that their eyesight had got into the hands of they could not guess whom. "Oh, what shall we do, sisters? what shall we do? We are all in the dark! Give us our eye! Give us our one, precious, solitary eye! You have two of your own! Give us our eye!"

"Tell them," whispered Quicksilver to Perseus, "that they shall have back the eye as soon as they direct you where to find

PLATE 2
Perseus and the Graiæ

the Nymphs who have the flying slippers, the magic wallet, and the helmet of darkness."

"My dear, good, admirable old ladies," said Perseus, addressing the Gray Women, "there is no occasion for putting yourselves into such a fright. I am by no means a bad young man. You shall have back your eye, safe and sound, and as bright as ever, the moment you tell me where to find the Nymphs."

"The Nymphs! Goodness me! sisters, what Nymphs does he mean?" screamed Scarecrow. "There are a great many Nymphs, people say; some that go a-hunting in the woods, and some that live inside of trees, and some that have a comfortable home in fountains of water. We know nothing at all about them. We are three unfortunate old souls, that go wandering about in the dusk, and never had but one eye amongst us, and that one you have stolen away. Oh, give it back, good stranger!—whoever you are, give it back!"

All this while the Three Gray Women were groping with their outstretched hands, and trying their utmost to get hold of Perseus. But he took good care to keep out of their reach.

"My respectable dames," said he,—for his mother had taught him always to use the greatest civility,—"I hold your eye fast in my hand, and shall keep it safely for you, until you please to tell me where to find these Nymphs. The Nymphs, I mean, who keep the enchanted wallet, the flying slippers, and the—what is it?— the helmet of invisibility."

"Mercy on us, sisters! what is the young man talking about?" exclaimed Scarecrow, Nightmare, and Shakejoint, one to another, with great appearance of astonishment. "A pair of flying slippers, quoth he! His heels would quickly fly higher than his head, if he were silly enough to put them on. And a helmet of invisibility! How could a helmet make him invisible, unless it were big enough for him to hide under it? And an enchanted wallet! What sort of a contrivance may that be, I wonder? No, no, good stranger! we can tell you nothing of these marvelous things. You have two eyes of your own, and we have but a single one amongst us three. You can find out such wonders better than three blind old creatures, like us."

Perseus, hearing them talk in this way, began really to think that the Gray Women knew nothing of the matter; and, as it grieved him to have put them to so much trouble, he was just on the point of restoring their eye and asking pardon for his rudeness in snatching it away. But Quicksilver caught his hand.

"Don't let them make a fool of you!" said he. "These Three Gray Women are the only persons in the world that can tell you where to find the Nymphs; and, unless you get that information, you will never succeed in cutting off the head of Medusa with the snaky locks. Keep fast hold of the eye, and all will go well."

As it turned out, Quicksilver was in the right. There are but few things that people prize so much as they do their eyesight; and the Gray Women valued their single eye as highly as if it had been half a dozen, which was the number they ought to have had. Finding that there was no other way of recovering it, they at last told Perseus what he wanted to know. No sooner had they done so, than he immediately, and with the utmost respect, clapped the eye into the vacant socket in one of their foreheads, thanked them for their kindness, and bade them farewell. Before the young man was out of hearing, however, they had got into a new dispute, because he happened to have given the eye to Scarecrow, who had already taken her turn of it when their trouble with Perseus commenced.

It is greatly to be feared that the Three Gray Women were very much in the habit of disturbing their mutual harmony by bickerings of this sort; which was the more pity, as they could not conveniently do without one another, and were evidently intended to be inseparable companions. As a general rule, I would advise all people, whether sisters or brothers, old or young, who chance to have but one eye amongst them, to cultivate forbearance, and not all insist upon peeping through it at once.

Quicksilver and Perseus, in the mean time, were making the best of their way in quest of the Nymphs. The old dames had given them such particular directions, that they were not long in finding them out. They proved to be very different persons from Nightmare, Shakejoint, and Scarecrow; for, instead of being old, they were young and beautiful; and instead of one eye amongst the sisterhood, each Nymph had two exceedingly bright eyes of her own, with which she looked very kindly at Perseus. They seemed to be acquainted with Quicksilver; and, when he told them the adventure which Perseus had undertaken, they made no difficulty about giving him the valuable articles that were in their custody. In the first place, they brought out what appeared to be a small purse, made of deerskin and curiously embroidered, and bade him be sure and keep it safe. This was the magic wallet. The Nymphs next produced a pair of shoes, or slippers, or sandals, with a nice little pair of wings at the heel of each.

"Put them on, Perseus," said Quicksilver. "You will find yourself as light-heeled as you can desire for the remainder of our journey."

So Perseus proceeded to put one of the slippers on, while he laid the other on the ground by his side. Unexpectedly, however, this other slipper spread its wings, fluttered up off the ground, and would probably have flown away, if Quicksilver had not made a leap, and luckily caught it in the air.

"Be more careful," said he, as he gave it back to Perseus. "It would frighten the birds, up aloft, if they should see a flying slipper amongst them."

When Perseus had got on both of these wonderful slippers, he was altogether too buoyant to tread on earth. Making a step or two, lo and behold! upward he popped into the air, high above the heads of Quicksilver and the Nymphs, and found it very difficult to clamber down again. Winged slippers, and all such high-flying contrivances, are seldom quite easy to manage until one grows a little accustomed to them. Quicksilver laughed at his companion's involuntary activity, and told him that he must not be in so desperate a hurry, but must wait for the invisible helmet.

The good-natured Nymphs had the helmet, with its dark tuft of waving plumes, all in readiness to put upon his head. And now there happened about as wonderful an incident as anything that I have yet told you. The instant before the helmet was put on, there stood Perseus, a beautiful young man, with golden ringlets and rosy cheeks, the crooked sword by his side, and the brightly polished shield upon his arm,—a figure that seemed all made up of courage, sprightliness, and glorious light. But when the helmet had descended over his white brow, there was no longer any Perseus to be seen! Nothing but empty air! Even the helmet, that covered him with its invisibility, had vanished!

PLATE 3
Perseus armed by the Nymphs

"Where are you, Perseus?" asked Quicksilver.

"Why, here, to be sure!" answered Perseus, very quietly, although his voice seemed to come out of the transparent atmosphere. "Just where I was a moment ago. Don't you see me?"

"No, indeed!" answered his friend. "You are hidden under the helmet. But, if I cannot see you, neither can the Gorgons. Follow me, therefore, and we will try your dexterity in using the winged slippers."

With these words, Quicksilver's cap spread its wings, as if his head were about to fly away from his shoulders; but his whole figure rose lightly into the air, and Perseus followed. By the time they had ascended a few hundred feet, the young man began to feel what a delightful thing it was to leave the dull earth so far beneath him, and to be able to flit about like a bird.

It was now deep night. Perseus looked upward, and saw the round, bright, silvery moon, and thought that he should desire nothing better than to soar up thither, and spend his life there. Then he looked downward again, and saw the earth, with its seas and lakes, and the silver courses of its rivers, and its snowy mountain-peaks, and the breadth of its fields, and the dark cluster of its woods, and its cities of white marble; and, with the moonshine sleeping over the whole scene, it was as beautiful as the moon or any star could be. And, among other objects, he saw the island of Seriphus, where his dear mother was. Sometimes he and Quicksilver approached a cloud that, at a distance, looked as if it were made of fleecy silver; although, when they plunged into it, they found themselves chilled and moistened with gray mist. So swift was their flight, however, that, in an instant, they emerged from the cloud into the moonlight again. Once, a high-soaring eagle flew right against the invisible Perseus. The bravest sights were the meteors, that gleamed suddenly out, as if a bonfire had been kindled in the sky, and made the moonshine pale for as much as a hundred miles around them.

As the two companions flew onward, Perseus fancied that he could hear the rustle of a garment close by his side; and it was on the side opposite to the one where he beheld Quicksilver, yet only Quicksilver was visible.

"Whose garment is this," inquired Perseus, "that keeps rustling close beside me in the breeze?"

"Oh, it is my sister's!" answered Quicksilver. "She is coming along with us, as I told you she would. We could do nothing without the help of my sister. You have no idea how wise she is. She has such eyes, too! Why, she can see you, at this moment, just as distinctly as if you were not invisible; and I'll venture to say, she will be the first to discover the Gorgons."

By this time, in their swift voyage through the air, they had come within sight of the great ocean, and were soon flying over it. Far beneath them, the waves tossed themselves tumultuously in mid-sea, or rolled a white surf-line upon the long beaches, or foamed against the rocky cliffs, with a roar that was thunderous, in the lower world; although it became a gentle murmur, like the voice of a baby half asleep, before it reached the ears of Perseus. Just then a voice spoke in the air close by him. It seemed to be a woman's voice, and was melodious, though not exactly what might be called sweet, but grave and mild.

"Perseus," said the voice, "there are the Gorgons."

"Where?" exclaimed Perseus. "I cannot see them."

"On the shore of that island beneath you," replied the voice. "A pebble, dropped from your hand, would strike in the midst of them."

"I told you she would be the first to discover them," said Quicksilver to Perseus. "And there they are!"

Straight downward, two or three thousand feet below him, Perseus perceived a small island, with the sea breaking into white foam all around its rocky shore, except on one side, where there was a beach of snowy sand. He descended towards it, and, looking earnestly at a cluster or heap of brightness, at the foot of a precipice of black rocks, behold, there were the terrible Gorgons! They lay fast asleep, soothed by the thunder of the sea; for it required a tumult that would have deafened everybody else to lull such fierce creatures into slumber. The moonlight glistened on their steely scales, and on their golden wings, which drooped idly over the sand. Their brazen claws, horrible to look at, were thrust out, and clutched the wave-beaten fragments of rock, while the sleeping Gorgons dreamed of tearing some poor mortal all to pieces. The snakes that served them instead of hair seemed likewise to be asleep; although, now and then, one would writhe, and lift its head, and thrust out its forked tongue, emitting a drowsy hiss, and then let itself subside among its sister snakes.

The Gorgons were more like an awful, gigantic kind of insect,—immense, golden-winged beetles, or dragon-flies, or things of that sort,—at once ugly and beautiful,—than like anything else; only that they were a thousand and a million times as big. And, with all this, there was something partly human about them, too. Luckily for Perseus, their faces were completely hidden from him by the posture in which they lay; for, had he but looked one instant at them, he would have fallen heavily out of the air, an image of senseless stone.

"Now," whispered Quicksilver, as he hovered by the side of Perseus,—"now is your time to do the deed! Be quick; for, if one of the Gorgons should awake, you are too late!"

"Which shall I strike at?" asked Perseus, drawing his sword and descending a little lower. "They all three look alike. All three have snaky locks. Which of the three is Medusa?"

It must be understood that Medusa was the only one of these dragon-monsters whose head Perseus could possibly cut off. As for the other two, let him have the sharpest sword that ever was forged, and he might have hacked away by the hour together, without doing them the least harm.

"Be cautious," said the calm voice which had before spoken to him. "One of the Gorgons is stirring in her sleep, and is just about to turn over. That is Medusa. Do not look at her! The sight would turn you to stone! Look at the reflection of her face and figure in the bright mirror of your shield."

Perseus now understood Quicksilver's motive for so earnestly exhorting him to polish his shield. In its surface he could safely look at the reflection of the Gorgon's face. And there it was,—that terrible countenance,—mirrored in the brightness of the shield, with the moonlight falling over it, and displaying all its horror. The snakes, whose venomous natures could not altogether sleep, kept twisting themselves over the forehead. It was the fiercest and most horrible face that ever was seen or imagined, and yet with a strange, fearful, and savage kind of beauty in it. The eyes were closed, and the Gorgon was still in a deep slumber; but there was an unquiet expression disturbing her features, as if the monster was troubled with an ugly dream. She gnashed her white tusks, and dug into the sand with her brazen claws.

The snakes, too, seemed to feel Medusa's dream, and to be made more restless by it. They twined themselves into tumultuous knots, writhed fiercely, and uplifted a hundred hissing heads, without opening their eyes.

"Now, now!" whispered Quicksilver, who was growing impatient. "Make a dash at the monster!"

"But be calm," said the grave, melodious voice at the young man's side. "Look in your shield, as you fly downward, and take care that you do not miss your first stroke."

Perseus flew cautiously downward, still keeping his eyes on Medusa's face, as reflected in his shield. The nearer he came, the more terrible did the snaky visage and metallic body of the monster grow. At last, when he found himself hovering over her within arm's length, Perseus uplifted his sword, while, at the same instant, each separate snake upon the Gorgon's head stretched threateningly upward, and Medusa unclosed her eyes. But she awoke too late. The sword was sharp; the stroke fell like a lightning-flash; and the head of the wicked Medusa tumbled from her body!

"Admirably done!" cried Quicksilver. "Make haste, and clap the head into your magic wallet."

To the astonishment of Perseus, the small embroidered wallet, which he had hung about his neck, and which had hitherto been no bigger than a purse, grew all at once large enough to contain Medusa's head. As quick as thought, he snatched it up, with the snakes still writhing upon it, and thrust it in.

PLATE 4
Perseus and the Gorgons

"Your task is done," said the calm voice. "Now fly; for the other Gorgons will do their utmost to take vengeance for Medusa's death."

It was, indeed, necessary to take flight; for Perseus had not done the deed so quietly but that the clash of his sword, and the hissing of the snakes, and the thump of Medusa's head as it tumbled upon the sea-beaten sand, awoke the other two monsters. There they sat, for an instant, sleepily rubbing their eyes with their brazen fingers, while all the snakes on their heads reared themselves on end with surprise, and with venomous malice against they knew not what. But when the Gorgons saw the scaly carcass of Medusa, headless, and her golden wings all ruffled, and half spread out on the sand, it was really awful to hear what yells and screeches they set up. And then the snakes! They sent forth a hundred-fold hiss, with one consent, and Medusa's snakes answered them out of the magic wallet.

No sooner were the Gorgons broad awake than they hurtled upward into the air, brandishing their brass talons, gnashing their horrible tusks, and flapping their huge wings so wildly that some of the golden feathers were shaken out, and floated down upon the shore. And there, perhaps, those very feathers lie scattered, till this day. Up rose the Gorgons, as I tell you, staring horribly about, in hopes of turning somebody to stone. Had Perseus looked them in the face, or had he fallen into their clutches, his poor mother would never have kissed her boy again! But he took good care to turn his eyes another way; and, as he wore the helmet of invisibility, the Gorgons knew not in what direction to follow him; nor did he fail to make the best use of the winged slippers, by soaring upward a perpendicular mile or so. At that height, when the screams of those abominable creatures sounded faintly beneath him, he made a straight course for the island of Seriphus, in order to carry Medusa's head to King Polydectes.

I have no time to tell you of several marvelous things that befell Perseus, on his way homeward; such as his killing a hideous sea-monster, just as it was on the point of devouring a beautiful maiden; nor how he changed an enormous giant into a mountain of stone, merely by showing him the head of the Gorgon. If you doubt this latter story, you may make a voyage to Africa, some day or other, and see the very mountain, which is still known by the ancient giant's name.

Finally, our brave Perseus arrived at the island, where he expected to see his dear mother. But, during his absence, the wicked king had treated Danaë so very ill that she was compelled to make her escape, and had taken refuge in a temple, where some good old priests were extremely kind to her. These praiseworthy priests, and the kind-hearted fisherman, who had first shown hospitality to Danaë and little Perseus when he found them afloat in the chest, seem to have been the only persons on the island who cared about doing right. All the rest of the people, as well as King Polydectes himself, were remarkably ill-behaved, and deserved no better destiny than that which was now to happen.

Not finding his mother at home, Perseus went straight to the palace, and was immediately ushered into the presence of the king. Polydectes was by no means rejoiced to see him; for he had felt almost certain, in his own evil mind, that the Gorgons would have torn the poor young man to pieces, and have eaten him up, out of the way. However, seeing him safely returned, he put the best face he could upon the matter and asked Perseus how he had succeeded.

"Have you performed your promise?" inquired he. "Have you brought me the head of Medusa with the snaky locks? If not, young man, it will cost you dear; for I must have a bridal present for the beautiful Princess Hippodamia, and there is nothing else that she would admire so much."

"Yes, please your Majesty," answered Perseus, in a quiet way, as if it were no very wonderful deed for such a young man as he to perform. "I have brought you the Gorgon's head, snaky locks and all!"

"Indeed! Pray let me see it," quoth King Polydectes. "It must be a very curious spectacle, if all that travelers tell about it be true!"

"Your Majesty is in the right," replied Perseus. "It is really an object that will be pretty certain to fix the regards of all who look at it. And, if your Majesty think fit, I would suggest that a holiday be proclaimed, and that all your Majesty's subjects be summoned to behold this wonderful curiosity. Few of them, I imagine, have seen a Gorgon's head before, and perhaps never may again!"

The king well knew that his subjects were an idle set of reprobates, and very fond of sight-seeing, as idle persons usually are. So he took the young man's advice, and sent out heralds and messengers, in all directions, to blow the trumpet at the street-corners, and in the market-places, and wherever two roads met, and summon everybody to court. Thither, accordingly, came a great multitude of good-for-nothing vagabonds, all of whom, out of pure love of mischief, would have been glad if Perseus had met with some ill-hap in his encounter with the Gorgons. If there were any better people in the island (as I really hope there may

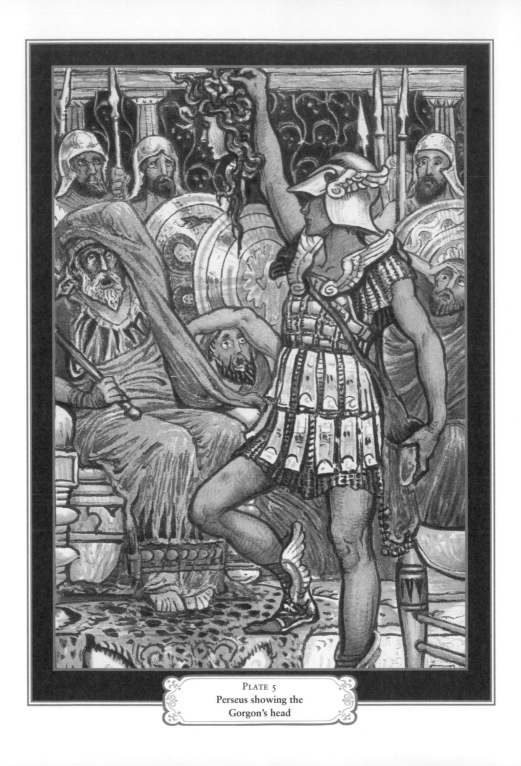

PLATE 5
Perseus showing the
Gorgon's head

have been, although the story tells nothing about any such), they stayed quietly at home, minding their business, and taking care of their little children. Most of the inhabitants, at all events, ran as fast as they could to the palace, and shoved, and pushed, and elbowed one another, in their eagerness to get near a balcony, on which Perseus showed himself, holding the embroidered wallet in his hand.

On a platform, within full view of the balcony, sat the mighty King Polydectes, amid his evil counselors, and with his flattering courtiers in a semicircle round about him. Monarch, counselors, courtiers, and subjects, all gazed eagerly towards Perseus.

"Show us the head! Show us the head!" shouted the people; and there was a fierceness in their cry as if they would tear Perseus to pieces, unless he should satisfy them with what he had to show. "Show us the head of Medusa with the snaky locks!"

A feeling of sorrow and pity came over the youthful Perseus.

"O King Polydectes," cried he, "and ye many people, I am very loath to show you the Gorgon's head!"

"Ah, the villain and coward!" yelled the people, more fiercely than before. "He is making game of us! He has no Gorgon's head! Show us the head, if you have it, or we will take your own head for a football!"

The evil counselors whispered bad advice in the king's ear; the courtiers murmured, with one consent, that Perseus had shown disrespect to their royal lord and master; and the great King Polydectes himself waved his hand, and ordered him, with the stern, deep voice of authority, on his peril, to produce the head.

"Show me the Gorgon's head, or I will cut off your own!"
And Perseus sighed.

"This instant," repeated Polydectes, "or you die!"

"Behold it, then!" cried Perseus, in a voice like the blast of a trumpet.

And, suddenly holding up the head, not an eyelid had time to wink before the wicked King Polydectes, his evil counselors, and all his fierce subjects were no longer anything but the mere images of a monarch and his people. They were all fixed, forever, in the look and attitude of that moment! At the first glimpse of the terrible head of Medusa, they whitened into marble! And Perseus thrust the head back into his wallet, and went to tell his dear mother that she need no longer be afraid of the wicked King Polydectes.

WAS NOT THAT A VERY FINE STORY?" ASKED EUSTACE.

"Oh, yes, yes!" cried Cowslip, clapping her hands. "And those funny old women, with only one eye amongst them! I never heard of anything so strange."

"As to their one tooth, which they shifted about," observed Primrose, "there was nothing so very wonderful in that. I suppose it was a false tooth. But think of your turning Mercury into Quicksilver, and talking about his sister! You are too ridiculous!"

"And was she not his sister?" asked Eustace Bright. "If I had thought of it sooner, I would have described her as a maiden lady, who kept a pet owl!"

"Well, at any rate," said Primrose, "your story seems to have driven away the mist."

And, indeed, while the tale was going forward, the vapors had been quite exhaled from the landscape. A scene was now disclosed which the spectators might almost fancy as having been created since they had last looked in the direction where it lay. About half a mile distant, in the lap of the valley, now appeared a beautiful lake, which reflected a perfect image of its own wooded banks, and of the summits of the more distant hills. It gleamed in glassy tranquillity, without the trace of a winged breeze on any part of its bosom. Beyond its farther shore was Monument Mountain, in a recumbent position, stretching almost across the valley. Eustace Bright compared it to a huge, headless sphinx, wrapped in a Persian shawl; and, indeed, so rich and diversified was the autumnal foliage of its woods, that the simile of the shawl was by no means too high-colored for the reality. In the lower ground, between Tanglewood and the lake, the clumps of trees and borders of woodland were chiefly golden-leaved or dusky brown, as having suffered more from frost than the foliage on the hill-sides.

Over all this scene there was a genial sunshine, intermingled with a slight haze, which made it unspeakably soft and tender. Oh, what a day of Indian summer was it going to be! The children snatched their baskets, and set forth, with hop, skip, and jump, and all sorts of frisks and gambols; while Cousin Eustace proved his fitness to preside over the party, by outdoing all their antics, and performing several new capers, which none of them could ever hope to imitate. Behind went a good old dog, whose name was Ben. He was one of the most respectable and kind-hearted of quadrupeds, and probably felt it to be his duty not to trust the children away from their parents without some better guardian than this feather-brained Eustace Bright.

INTRODUCTORY TO THE GOLDEN TOUCH

T NOON, OUR JUVENILE PARTY assembled in a dell, through the depths of which ran a little brook. The dell was narrow, and its steep sides, from the margin of the stream upward, were thickly set with trees, chiefly walnuts and chestnuts, among which grew a few oaks and maples. In the summer time, the shade of so many clustering branches, meeting and intermingling across the rivulet, was deep enough to produce a noontide twilight. Hence came the name of Shadow Brook. But now, ever since autumn had crept into this secluded place, all the dark verdure was changed to gold, so that it really kindled up the dell, instead of shading it. The bright yellow leaves, even had it been a cloudy day, would have seemed to keep the sunlight among them; and enough of them had fallen to strew all the bed and margin of the brook with sunlight, too. Thus the shady nook, where summer had cooled herself, was now the sunniest spot anywhere to be found.

The little brook ran along over its pathway of gold, here pausing to form a pool, in which minnows were darting to and fro; and then it hurried onward at a swifter pace, as if in haste to reach the lake; and, forgetting to look whither it went, it tumbled over the root of a tree, which stretched quite across its current. You would have laughed to hear how noisily it babbled about this accident. And even after it had run onward, the brook still kept talking to itself, as if it were in a maze. It was wonder-smitten, I suppose, at finding its dark dell so illuminated, and at hearing the prattle and merriment of so many children. So it stole away as quickly as it could, and hid itself in the lake.

In the dell of Shadow Brook, Eustace Bright and his little friends had eaten their dinner. They had brought plenty of good things from Tanglewood, in their baskets, and had spread them out on the stumps of trees and on mossy trunks, and had feasted merrily, and made a very nice dinner indeed. After it was over, nobody felt like stirring.

"We will rest ourselves here," said several of the children, "while Cousin Eustace tells us another of his pretty stories."

Cousin Eustace had a good right to be tired, as well as the children, for he had performed great feats on that memorable forenoon. Dandelion, Clover, Cowslip, and Buttercup were almost persuaded that he had winged slippers, like those which the Nymphs gave Perseus; so often had the student shown himself at the tiptop of a nut-tree, when only a moment before he had been standing on the ground. And then, what showers of walnuts had he sent rattling down upon their heads, for their busy little hands to gather into the baskets! In short, he had been as active as a squirrel or a monkey, and now, flinging himself down on the yellow leaves, seemed inclined to take a little rest.

But children have no mercy nor consideration for anybody's weariness; and if you had but a single breath left, they would ask you to spend it in telling them a story.

"Cousin Eustace," said Cowslip, "that was a very nice story of the Gorgon's Head. Do you think you could tell us another as good?"

"Yes, child," said Eustace, pulling the brim of his cap over his eyes, as if preparing for a nap. "I can tell you a dozen, as good or better, if I choose."

"O Primrose and Periwinkle, do you hear what he says?" cried Cowslip, dancing with delight. "Cousin Eustace is going to tell us a dozen better stories than that about the Gorgon's Head!"

"I did not promise you even one, you foolish little Cowslip!" said Eustace, half pettishly. "However, I suppose you must have it. This is the consequence of having earned a reputation! I wish I were a great deal duller than I am, or that I had never shown half the bright qualities with which nature has endowed me; and then I might have my nap out, in peace and comfort!"

But Cousin Eustace, as I think I have hinted before, was as fond of telling his stories as the children of hearing them. His mind was in a free and happy state, and took delight in its own activity, and scarcely required any external impulse to set it at work.

How different is this spontaneous play of the intellect from the trained diligence of maturer years, when toil has perhaps grown easy by long habit, and the day's work may have become essential to the day's comfort, although the rest of the matter has bubbled away! This remark, however, is not meant for the children to hear.

Without further solicitation, Eustace Bright proceeded to tell the following really splendid story. It had come into his mind as he lay looking upward into the depths of a tree, and observing how the touch of Autumn had transmuted every one of its green leaves into what resembled the purest gold. And this change, which we have all of us witnessed, is as wonderful as anything that Eustace told about in the story of Midas.

THE GOLDEN TOUCH

NCE UPON A TIME, THERE LIVED A VERY rich man, and a king besides, whose name was Midas; and he had a little daughter, whom nobody but myself ever heard of, and whose name I either never knew, or have entirely forgotten. So, because I love odd names for little girls, I choose to call her Marygold.

This King Midas was fonder of gold than of anything else in the world. He valued his royal crown chiefly because it was composed of that precious metal. If he loved anything better, or half so well, it was the one little maiden who played so merrily around her father's footstool. But the more Midas loved his daughter, the more did he desire and seek for wealth. He thought, foolish man! that the best thing he could possibly do for this dear child would be to bequeath her the immensest pile of yellow, glistening coin, that had ever been heaped together since the world was made. Thus, he gave all his thoughts and all his time to this one purpose. If ever he happened to gaze for an instant at the gold-tinted clouds of sunset, he wished that they were real gold, and that they could be squeezed safely into his strong box. When little Marygold ran to meet him, with a bunch of buttercups and dandelions, he used to say, "Poh, poh, child! If these flowers were as golden as they look, they would be worth the plucking!"

And yet, in his earlier days, before he was so entirely possessed of this insane desire for riches, King Midas had shown a great taste for flowers. He had planted a garden, in which grew the biggest and beautifullest and sweetest roses that any mortal ever saw or smelt. These roses were still growing in the garden, as large, as lovely, and as fragrant, as when Midas used to pass whole hours in gazing at them, and inhaling their perfume. But now, if he looked at them at all, it was only to calculate how much the garden would be worth if each of the innumerable rose-petals were a thin plate of gold. And though he once was fond of music (in spite of an idle story about his ears, which were said to resemble those of an ass), the only music for poor Midas, now, was the chink of one coin against another.

At length (as people always grow more and more foolish, unless they take care to grow wiser and wiser), Midas had got to be so exceedingly unreasonable, that he could scarcely bear to see or touch any object that was not gold. He made it his custom, therefore, to pass a large portion of every day in a dark and dreary apartment, under ground, at the basement of his palace. It was here that he kept his wealth. To this dismal hole—for it was little better than a dungeon—Midas betook himself, whenever he wanted to be particularly happy. Here, after carefully locking the door, he would take a bag of gold coin, or a gold cup as big as a washbowl, or a heavy golden bar, or a peck-measure of gold-dust, and bring them from the obscure corners of the room into the one bright and narrow sunbeam that fell from the dungeon-like window. He valued the sunbeam for no other reason but that his treasure would not shine without its help. And then would he reckon over the coins in the bag; toss up the bar, and catch it as it came down; sift the gold-dust through his fingers; look at the funny image of his own face, as reflected in the burnished circumference of the cup; and whisper to himself, "O Midas, rich King Midas, what a happy man art thou!" But it was laughable to see how the image of his face kept grinning at him, out of the polished surface of the cup. It seemed to be aware of his foolish behavior, and to have a naughty inclination to make fun of him.

Midas called himself a happy man, but felt that he was not yet quite so happy as he might be. The very tiptop of enjoyment would never be reached, unless the whole world were to become his treasure-room, and be filled with yellow metal which should be all his own.

Now, I need hardly remind such wise little people as you are, that in the old, old times, when King Midas was alive, a great many things came to pass, which we should consider wonderful if they were to happen in our own day and country. And, on the other hand, a great many things take place nowadays, which seem not only wonderful to us, but at which the people of old times would have stared their eyes out. On the whole, I regard our own times as the strangest of the two; but, however that may be, I must go on with my story.

Midas was enjoying himself in his treasure-room, one day, as usual, when he perceived a shadow fall over the heaps of gold; and, looking suddenly up, what should he behold but the figure of a stranger, standing in the bright and narrow sunbeam! It was a young man, with a cheerful and ruddy face. Whether it was that the imagination of King Midas threw a yellow tinge over everything, or whatever the cause might be, he could not help fancying that the smile with which the stranger regarded him had a kind of golden radiance in it. Certainly, although his figure intercepted the sunshine, there was now a brighter gleam upon all the piled-up treasures than before. Even the remotest corners had their share of it, and were lighted up, when the stranger smiled, as with tips of flame and sparkles of fire.

As Midas knew that he had carefully turned the key in the lock, and that no mortal strength could possibly break into his treasure-room, he, of course, concluded that his visitor must be something more than mortal. It is no matter about telling you who he was. In those days, when the earth was comparatively a new affair, it was supposed to be often the resort of beings endowed with supernatural power, and who used to interest themselves in the joys and sorrows of men, women, and children, half playfully and half seriously. Midas had met such beings before now, and was not sorry to meet one of them again. The stranger's aspect, indeed, was so good-humored and kindly, if not beneficent, that it would have been unreasonable to suspect him of intending any mischief. It was far more probable that he came to do Midas a favor. And what could that favor be, unless to multiply his heaps of treasure?

The stranger gazed about the room; and when his lustrous smile had glistened upon all the golden objects that were there, he turned again to Midas.

PLATE 6
The stranger appearing to Midas

"You are a wealthy man, friend Midas!" he observed. "I doubt whether any other four walls, on earth, contain so much gold as you have contrived to pile up in this room."

"I have done pretty well,—pretty well," answered Midas, in a discontented tone. "But, after all, it is but a trifle, when you consider that it has taken me my whole life to get it together. If one could live a thousand years, he might have time to grow rich!"

"What!" exclaimed the stranger. "Then you are not satisfied?"

Midas shook his head.

"And pray what would satisfy you?" asked the stranger. "Merely for the curiosity of the thing, I should be glad to know."

Midas paused and meditated. He felt a presentiment that this stranger, with such a golden lustre in his good-humored smile, had come hither with both the power and the purpose of gratifying his utmost wishes. Now, therefore, was the fortunate moment, when he had but to speak, and obtain whatever possible, or seemingly impossible thing, it might come into his head to ask. So he thought, and thought, and thought, and heaped up one golden mountain upon another, in his imagination, without being able to imagine them big enough. At last, a bright idea occurred to King Midas. It seemed really as bright as the glistening metal which he loved so much.

Raising his head, he looked the lustrous stranger in the face.

"Well, Midas," observed his visitor, "I see that you have at length hit upon something that will satisfy you. Tell me your wish."

"It is only this," replied Midas. "I am weary of collecting my treasures with so much trouble, and beholding the heap so diminutive, after I have done my best. I wish everything that I touch to be changed to gold!"

The stranger's smile grew so very broad, that it seemed to fill the room like an outburst of the sun, gleaming into a shadowy dell, where the yellow autumnal leaves—for so looked the lumps and particles of gold—lie strewn in the glow of light.

"The Golden Touch!" exclaimed he. "You certainly deserve credit, friend Midas, for striking out so brilliant a conception. But are you quite sure that this will satisfy you?"

"How could it fail?" said Midas.

"And will you never regret the possession of it?"

"What could induce me?" asked Midas. "I ask nothing else, to render me perfectly happy."

"Be it as you wish, then," replied the stranger, waving his hand in token of farewell. "To-morrow, at sunrise, you will find yourself gifted with the Golden Touch."

The figure of the stranger then became exceedingly bright, and Midas involuntarily closed his eyes. On opening them again, he beheld only one yellow sunbeam in the room, and, all around him, the glistening of the precious metal which he had spent his life in hoarding up.

Whether Midas slept as usual that night, the story does not say. Asleep or awake, however, his mind was probably in the state of a child's, to whom a beautiful new plaything has been promised in the morning. At any rate, day had hardly peeped over the hills, when King Midas was broad awake, and, stretching his arms out of bed, began to touch the objects that were within reach. He was anxious to prove whether the Golden Touch had really come, according to the stranger's promise. So he laid his finger on a chair by the bedside, and on various other things, but was grievously disappointed to perceive that they remained of exactly the same substance as before. Indeed, he felt very much afraid that he had only dreamed about the lustrous stranger, or else that the latter had been making game of him. And what a miserable affair would it be, if, after all his hopes, Midas must content himself with what little gold he could scrape together by ordinary means, instead of creating it by a touch!

All this while, it was only the gray of the morning, with but a streak of brightness along the edge of the sky, where Midas could not see it. He lay in a very disconsolate mood, regretting the downfall of his hopes, and kept growing sadder and sadder, until the earliest sunbeam shone through the window, and gilded the ceiling over his head. It seemed to Midas that this bright yellow sunbeam was reflected in rather a singular way on the white covering of the bed. Looking more closely, what was his astonishment and delight, when he found that this linen fabric had been transmuted to what seemed a woven texture of the purest and brightest gold! The Golden Touch had come to him with the first sunbeam!

Midas started up, in a kind of joyful frenzy, and ran about the room, grasping at everything that happened to be in his way. He seized one of the bed-posts, and it became immediately a fluted golden pillar. He pulled aside a window-curtain, in order to admit a clear spectacle of the wonders which he was performing; and the tassel grew heavy in his hand,—a mass of gold. He took up a book from the table. At his first touch, it assumed the appearance of such a splendidly bound and gilt-edged volume as one often meets with, nowadays; but, on running his fingers through the leaves, behold! it was a bundle of thin golden plates, in which all the wisdom of the book had grown illegible. He hurriedly put on his clothes, and was enraptured to see himself in a magnificent suit of gold cloth, which retained its flexibility and softness, although it burdened him a little with its weight. He drew out his handkerchief, which little Marygold had hemmed for him. That was likewise gold, with the dear child's neat and pretty stitches running all along the border, in gold thread!

Somehow or other, this last transformation did not quite please King Midas. He would rather that his little daughter's handiwork should have remained just the same as when she climbed his knee and put it into his hand.

But it was not worth while to vex himself about a trifle. Midas now took his spectacles from his pocket, and put them on his nose, in order that he might see more distinctly what he was about. In those days, spectacles for common people had not been invented, but were already worn by kings; else, how could Midas have had any? To his great perplexity, however, excellent as the glasses were, he discovered that he could not possibly see through them. But this was the most natural thing in the world; for, on taking them off, the transparent crystal turned out to be plates of yellow metal, and, of course, were worthless as spectacles, though valuable as gold. It struck Midas as rather inconvenient that, with all his wealth, he could never again be rich enough to own a pair of serviceable spectacles.

"It is no great matter, nevertheless," said he to himself, very philosophically. "We cannot expect any great good, without its being accompanied with some small inconvenience. The Golden Touch is worth the sacrifice of a pair of spectacles, at least, if not of one's very eyesight. My own eyes will serve for ordinary purposes, and little Marygold will soon be old enough to read to me."

Wise King Midas was so exalted by his good fortune, that the palace seemed not sufficiently spacious to contain him. He therefore went downstairs, and smiled, on observing that the balustrade of the staircase became a bar of burnished gold, as his hand passed over it, in his descent. He lifted the door-latch (it was brass only a moment ago, but golden when his fingers quitted it), and emerged into the garden. Here, as it happened, he found a great number of beautiful roses in full bloom, and others in all the stages of lovely bud and blossom. Very delicious was their fragrance in the morning breeze. Their delicate blush was one of the fairest sights in the world; so gentle, so modest, and so full of sweet tranquillity, did these roses seem to be.

But Midas knew a way to make them far more precious, according to his way of thinking, than roses had ever been before. So he took great pains in going from bush to bush, and exercised his magic touch most indefatigably; until every individual flower and bud, and even the worms at the heart of some of them, were changed to gold. By the time this good work was completed, King Midas was summoned to breakfast; and as the morning air had given him an excellent appetite, he made haste back to the palace.

What was usually a king's breakfast in the days of Midas, I really do not know, and cannot stop now to investigate. To the best of my belief, however, on this particular morning, the breakfast consisted of hot cakes, some nice little brook trout, roasted potatoes, fresh boiled eggs, and coffee, for King Midas himself, and a bowl of bread and milk for his daughter Marygold. At all events, this is a breakfast fit to set before a king; and, whether he had it or not, King Midas could not have had a better.

Little Marygold had not yet made her appearance. Her father ordered her to be called, and, seating himself at table, awaited the child's coming, in order to begin his own breakfast. To do Midas justice, he really loved his daughter, and loved her so much the more this morning, on account of the good fortune which had befallen him. It was not a great while before he heard her coming along the passageway crying bitterly. This circumstance surprised him, because Marygold was one of the cheerfullest little people whom you would see in a summer's day, and hardly shed a thimbleful of tears in a twelvemonth. When Midas heard her sobs, he determined to put little Marygold into better spirits, by an agreeable surprise; so, leaning across the table, he touched his daughter's bowl (which was a China one, with pretty figures all around it), and transmuted it to gleaming gold.

Meanwhile, Marygold slowly and disconsolately opened the door, and showed herself with her apron at her eyes, still sobbing as if her heart would break.

"How now, my little lady!" cried Midas. "Pray what is the matter with you, this bright morning?"

Marygold, without taking the apron from her eyes, held out her hand, in which was one of the roses which Midas had so recently transmuted.

"Beautiful!" exclaimed her father. "And what is there in this magnificent golden rose to make you cry?"

"Ah, dear father!" answered the child, as well as her sobs would let her; "it is not beautiful, but the ugliest flower that ever grew! As soon as I was dressed I ran into the garden to gather some roses for you; because I know you like them, and like them the better when gathered by your little daughter. But, oh dear,

dear me! What do you think has happened? Such a misfortune! All the beautiful roses, that smelled so sweetly and had so many lovely blushes, are blighted and spoilt! They are grown quite yellow, as you see this one, and have no longer any fragrance! What can have been the matter with them?"

"Poh, my dear little girl,—pray don't cry about it!" said Midas, who was ashamed to confess that he himself had wrought the change which so greatly afflicted her. "Sit down and eat your bread and milk! You will find it easy enough to exchange a golden rose like that (which will last hundreds of years) for an ordinary one which would wither in a day."

"I don't care for such roses as this!" cried Marygold, tossing it contemptuously away. "It has no smell, and the hard petals prick my nose!"

The child now sat down to table, but was so occupied with her grief for the blighted roses that she did not even notice the wonderful transmutation of her China bowl. Perhaps this was all the better; for Marygold was accustomed to take pleasure in looking at the queer figures, and strange trees and houses, that were painted on the circumference of the bowl; and these ornaments were now entirely lost in the yellow hue of the metal.

Midas, meanwhile, had poured out a cup of coffee, and, as a matter of course, the coffee-pot, whatever metal it may have been when he took it up, was gold when he set it down. He thought to himself, that it was rather an extravagant style of splendor, in a king of his simple habits, to breakfast off a service of gold, and began to be puzzled with the difficulty of keeping his treasures safe. The cupboard and the kitchen would no longer be a secure place of deposit for articles so valuable as golden bowls and coffee-pots.

Amid these thoughts, he lifted a spoonful of coffee to his lips, and, sipping it, was astonished to perceive that, the instant his lips touched the liquid, it became molten gold, and, the next moment, hardened into a lump!

"Ha!" exclaimed Midas, rather aghast.

"What is the matter, father?" asked little Marygold, gazing at him, with the tears still standing in her eyes.

"Nothing, child, nothing!" said Midas. "Eat your milk, before it gets quite cold."

He took one of the nice little trouts on his plate, and, by way of experiment, touched its tail with his finger. To his horror, it was immediately transmuted from an admirably fried brook-trout into a gold-fish, though not one of those gold-fishes which people often keep in glass globes, as ornaments for the parlor. No; but it was really a metallic fish, and looked as if it had been very cunningly made by the nicest goldsmith in the world. Its little bones were now golden wires; its fins and tail were thin plates of gold; and there were the marks of the fork in it, and all the delicate, frothy appearance of a nicely fried fish, exactly imitated in metal. A very pretty piece of work, as you may suppose; only King Midas, just at that moment, would much rather have had a real trout in his dish than this elaborate and valuable imitation of one.

"I don't quite see," thought he to himself, "how I am to get any breakfast."

He took one of the smoking-hot cakes, and had scarcely broken it, when, to his cruel mortification, though, a moment before, it had been of the whitest wheat, it assumed the yellow hue of Indian meal. To say the truth, if it had really been a hot Indian cake, Midas would have prized it a good deal more than he now did, when its solidity and increased weight made him too bitterly sensible that it was gold. Almost in despair, he helped himself to a boiled egg, which immediately underwent a change similar to those of the trout and the cake. The egg, indeed, might have been mistaken for one of those which the famous goose, in the story-book, was in the habit of laying; but King Midas was the only goose that had anything to do with the matter.

"Well, this is a quandary!" thought he, leaning back in his chair, and looking quite enviously at little Marygold, who was now eating her bread and milk with great satisfaction. "Such a costly breakfast before me, and nothing that can be eaten!"

Hoping that, by dint of great dispatch, he might avoid what he now felt to be a considerable inconvenience, King Midas next snatched a hot potato, and attempted to cram it into his mouth, and swallow it in a hurry. But the Golden Touch was too nimble for him. He found his mouth full, not of mealy potato, but of solid metal, which so burnt his tongue that he roared aloud, and, jumping up from the table, began to dance and stamp about the room, both with pain and affright.

"Father, dear father!" cried little Marygold, who was a very affectionate child, "pray what is the matter? Have you burnt your mouth?"

"Ah, dear child," groaned Midas, dolefully, "I don't know what is to become of your poor father!"

And, truly, my dear little folks, did you ever hear of such a pitiable case in all your lives? Here was literally the richest breakfast that could be set before a king, and its very richness made it absolutely good for nothing. The poorest laborer, sitting down to his crust of bread and cup of water, was far better off than King Midas, whose delicate food was really worth its weight in gold. And what was to be done? Already, at breakfast, Midas was excessively hungry. Would he be less so by dinner time? And how ravenous would be his appetite for supper, which must undoubtedly consist of the same sort of indigestible dishes as those now before him! How many days, think you, would he survive a continuance of this rich fare?

These reflections so troubled wise King Midas, that he began to doubt whether, after all, riches are the one desirable thing in the world, or even the most desirable. But this was only a passing thought. So fascinated was Midas with the glitter of the yellow metal, that he would still have refused to give up the Golden Touch for so paltry a consideration as a breakfast. Just imagine what a price for one meal's victuals! It would have been the same as paying millions and millions of money (and as many millions more as would take forever to reckon up) for some fried trout, an egg, a potato, a hot cake, and a cup of coffee!

"It would be quite too dear," thought Midas.

Nevertheless, so great was his hunger, and the perplexity of his situation, that he again groaned aloud, and very grievously too. Our pretty Marygold could endure it no longer. She sat, a moment, gazing at her father, and trying, with all the might of her little wits, to find out what was the matter with him. Then, with a sweet and sorrowful impulse to comfort him, she started from her chair, and, running to Midas, threw her arms affectionately about his knees. He bent down and kissed her. He felt that his

PLATE 7
Midas' daughter turned to gold

little daughter's love was worth a thousand times more than he had gained by the Golden Touch.

"My precious, precious Marygold!" cried he.

But Marygold made no answer.

Alas, what had he done? How fatal was the gift which the stranger bestowed! The moment the lips of Midas touched Marygold's forehead, a change had taken place. Her sweet, rosy face, so full of affection as it had been, assumed a glittering yellow color, with yellow tear-drops congealing on her cheeks. Her beautiful brown ringlets took the same tint. Her soft and tender little form grew hard and inflexible within her father's encircling arms. Oh, terrible misfortune! The victim of his insatiable desire for wealth, little Marygold was a human child no longer, but a golden statue!

Yes, there she was, with the questioning look of love, grief, and pity, hardened into her face. It was the prettiest and most woeful sight that ever mortal saw. All the features and tokens of Marygold were there; even the beloved little dimple remained in her golden chin. But the more perfect was the resemblance, the greater was the father's agony at beholding this golden image, which was all that was left him of a daughter. It had been a favorite phrase of Midas, whenever he felt particularly fond of the child, to say that she was worth her weight in gold. And now the phrase had become literally true. And now, at last, when it was too late, he felt how infinitely a warm and tender heart, that loved him, exceeded in value all the wealth that could be piled up betwixt the earth and sky!

It would be too sad a story, if I were to tell you how Midas, in the fullness of all his gratified desires, began to wring his hands and bemoan himself; and how he could neither bear to look at Marygold, nor yet to look away from her. Except when his eyes were fixed on the image, he could not possibly believe that she was changed to gold. But, stealing another glance, there was the precious little figure, with a yellow tear-drop on its yellow cheek, and a look so piteous and tender, that it seemed as if that very expression must needs soften the gold, and make it flesh again. This, however, could not be. So Midas had only to wring his hands, and to wish that he were the poorest man in the wide world, if the loss of all his wealth might bring back the faintest rose-color to his dear child's face.

While he was in this tumult of despair, he suddenly beheld a stranger standing near the door. Midas bent down his head, without speaking; for he recognized the same figure which had appeared to him, the day before, in the treasure-room, and had bestowed on him this disastrous faculty of the Golden Touch. The stranger's countenance still wore a smile, which seemed to shed a yellow lustre all about the room, and gleamed on little Marygold's image, and on the other objects that had been transmuted by the touch of Midas.

"Well, friend Midas," said the stranger, "pray how do you succeed with the Golden Touch?"

Midas shook his head.

"I am very miserable," said he.

"Very miserable, indeed!" exclaimed the stranger. "And how happens that? Have I not faithfully kept my promise with you? Have you not everything that your heart desired?"

"Gold is not everything," answered Midas. "And I have lost all that my heart really cared for."

"Ah! So you have made a discovery, since yesterday?" observed the stranger. "Let us see, then. Which of these two things do you think is really worth the most,—the gift of the Golden Touch, or one cup of clear cold water?"

"O blessed water!" exclaimed Midas. "It will never moisten my parched throat again!"

"The Golden Touch," continued the stranger, "or a crust of bread?"

"A piece of bread," answered Midas, "is worth all the gold on earth!"

"The Golden Touch," asked the stranger, "or your own little Marygold, warm, soft, and loving as she was an hour ago?"

"Oh, my child, my dear child!" cried poor Midas, wringing his hands. "I would not have given that one small dimple in her chin for the power of changing this whole big earth into a solid lump of gold!"

"You are wiser than you were, King Midas!" said the stranger, looking seriously at him. "Your own heart, I perceive, has not been entirely changed from flesh to gold. Were it so, your case would indeed be desperate. But you appear to be still capable of understanding that the commonest things, such as lie within everybody's grasp, are more valuable than the riches which so many mortals sigh and struggle after. Tell me, now, do you sincerely desire to rid yourself of this Golden Touch?"

"It is hateful to me!" replied Midas.

A fly settled on his nose, but immediately fell to the floor; for it, too, had become gold. Midas shuddered.

"Go, then," said the stranger, "and plunge into the river that glides past the bottom of your garden. Take likewise a vase of the same water, and sprinkle it over any object that you may desire to change back again from gold into its former substance. If you do this in earnestness and sincerity, it may possibly repair the mischief which your avarice has occasioned."

King Midas bowed low; and when he lifted his head, the lustrous stranger had vanished.

You will easily believe that Midas lost no time in snatching up a great earthen pitcher (but, alas me! it was no longer earthen after he touched it), and hastening to the river-side. As he scampered along, and forced his way through the shrubbery, it was positively marvelous to see how the foliage turned yellow behind him, as if the autumn had been there, and nowhere else. On reaching the river's brink, he plunged headlong in, without waiting so much as to pull off his shoes.

"Poof! poof! poof!" snorted King Midas, as his head emerged out of the water. "Well; this is really a refreshing bath, and I think it must have quite washed away the Golden Touch. And now for filling my pitcher!"

As he dipped the pitcher into the water, it gladdened his very heart to see it change from gold into the same good, honest earthen vessel which it had been before he touched it. He was conscious, also, of a change within himself. A cold, hard, and heavy weight seemed to have gone out of his bosom. No doubt, his heart had been gradually losing its human substance, and transmuting itself into insensible metal, but had now softened back again into flesh. Perceiving a violet, that grew on the bank of the river, Midas touched it with his finger, and was overjoyed to find that the delicate flower retained its purple hue, instead of undergoing a yellow blight. The curse of the Golden Touch had, therefore, really been removed from him.

PLATE 8
Midas with the pitcher

King Midas hastened back to the palace; and, I suppose, the servants knew not what to make of it when they saw their royal master so carefully bringing home an earthen pitcher of water. But that water, which was to undo all the mischief that his folly had wrought, was more precious to Midas than an ocean of molten gold could have been. The first thing he did, as you need hardly be told, was to sprinkle it by handfuls over the golden figure of little Marygold.

No sooner did it fall on her than you would have laughed to see how the rosy color came back to the dear child's cheek! and how she began to sneeze and sputter!—and how astonished she was to find herself dripping wet, and her father still throwing more water over her!

"Pray do not, dear father!" cried she. "See how you have wet my nice frock, which I put on only this morning!"

For Marygold did not know that she had been a little golden statue; nor could she remember anything that had happened since the moment when she ran with outstretched arms to comfort poor King Midas.

Her father did not think it necessary to tell his beloved child how very foolish he had been, but contented himself with showing how much wiser he had now grown. For this purpose, he led little Marygold into the garden, where he sprinkled all the remainder of the water over the rose-bushes, and with such good effect that above five thousand roses recovered their beautiful bloom. There were two circumstances, however, which, as long as he lived, used to put King Midas in mind of the Golden Touch. One was, that the sands of the river sparkled like gold; the other, that little Marygold's hair had now a golden tinge, which he had never observed in it before she had been transmuted by the effect of his kiss. This change of hue was really an improvement, and made Marygold's hair richer than in her babyhood.

When King Midas had grown quite an old man, and used to trot Marygold's children on his knee, he was fond of telling them this marvelous story, pretty much as I have now told it to you. And then would he stroke their glossy ringlets, and tell them that their hair, likewise, had a rich shade of gold, which they had inherited from their mother.

"And to tell you the truth, my precious little folks," quoth King Midas, diligently trotting the children all the while, "ever since that morning, I have hated the very sight of all other gold, save this!"

SHADOW·BROOK · AFTER · THE · STORY

ELL, CHILDREN," INQUIRED EUSTACE, who was very fond of eliciting a definite opinion from his auditors, "did you ever, in all your lives, listen to a better story than this of 'The Golden Touch'?"

"Why, as to the story of King Midas," said saucy Primrose, "it was a famous one thousands of years before Mr. Eustace Bright came into the world, and will continue to be so long after he quits it. But some people have what we may call 'The Leaden Touch,' and make everything dull and heavy that they lay their fingers upon."

"You are a smart child, Primrose, to be not yet in your teens," said Eustace, taken rather aback by the piquancy of her criticism. "But you well know, in your naughty little heart, that I have burnished the old gold of Midas all over anew, and have made it shine as it never shone before. And then that figure of Marygold! Do you perceive no nice workmanship in that? And how finely I have brought out and deepened the moral! What say you, Sweet Fern, Dandelion, Clover, Periwinkle? Would any of you, after hearing this story, be so foolish as to desire the faculty of changing things to gold?"

"I should like," said Periwinkle, a girl of ten, "to have the power of turning everything to gold with my right forefinger; but, with my left forefinger, I should want the power of changing it back again, if the first change did not please me. And I know what I would do, this very afternoon!"

"Pray tell me," said Eustace.

"Why," answered Periwinkle, "I would touch every one of these golden leaves on the trees with my left forefinger, and make them all green again; so that we might have the summer back at once, with no ugly winter in the mean time."

"O Periwinkle!" cried Eustace Bright, "there you are wrong, and would do a great deal of mischief. Were I Midas, I would make nothing else but just such golden days as these over and over again, all the year throughout. My best thoughts always come a little too late. Why did not I tell you how old King Midas came to America, and changed the dusky autumn, such as it is in other countries, into the burnished beauty which it here puts on? He gilded the leaves of the great volume of Nature."

"Cousin Eustace," said Sweet Fern, a good little boy, who was always making particular inquiries about the precise height of giants and the littleness of fairies, "how big was Marygold, and how much did she weigh after she was turned to gold?"

"She was about as tall as you are," replied Eustace, "and, as gold is very heavy, she weighed at least two thousand pounds, and might have been coined into thirty or forty thousand gold dollars. I wish Primrose were worth half as much. Come, little people, let us clamber out of the dell, and look about us."

They did so. The sun was now an hour or two beyond its noon-tide mark, and filled the great hollow of the valley with its western radiance, so that it seemed to be brimming with mellow light, and to spill it over the surrounding hill-sides, like golden wine out of a bowl. It was such a day that you could not help saying of it, "There never was such a day before!" although yesterday was just such a day, and to-morrow will be just such another. Ah, but there are very few of them in a twelvemonth's circle! It is a remarkable peculiarity of these October days, that each of them seems to occupy a great deal of space, although the sun rises rather tardily at that season of the year, and goes to bed, as little children ought, at sober six o'clock, or even earlier. We cannot, therefore, call the days long; but they appear, somehow or other, to make up for their shortness by their breadth; and when the cool night comes, we are conscious of having enjoyed a big armful of life, since morning.

"Come, children, come!" cried Eustace Bright. "More nuts, more nuts, more nuts! Fill all your baskets; and, at Christmas time, I will crack them for you, and tell you beautiful stories!"

So away they went; all of them in excellent spirits, except little Dandelion, who, I am sorry to tell you, had been sitting on a chestnut-bur, and was stuck as full as a pincushion of its prickles. Dear me, how uncomfortably he must have felt!

THE·PARADISE·OF·CHILDREN·

TANGLEWOOD PLAY-ROOM
INTRODUCTORY TO THE
PARADISE OF CHILDREN

HE GOLDEN DAYS OF OCTOBER PASSED away, as so many other Octobers have, and brown November likewise, and the greater part of chill December, too. At last came merry Christmas, and Eustace Bright along with it, making it all the merrier by his presence. And, the day after his arrival from college, there came a mighty snow-storm. Up to this time, the winter had held back, and had given us a good many mild days, which were like smiles upon its wrinkled visage. The grass had kept itself green, in sheltered places, such as the nooks of southern hill-slopes, and along the lee of the stone fences. It was but a week or two ago, and since the beginning of the month, that the children had found a dandelion in bloom, on the margin of Shadow Brook, where it glides out of the dell.

But no more green grass and dandelions now. This was such a snow-storm! Twenty miles of it might have been visible at once, between the windows of Tanglewood and the dome of Taconic, had it been possible to see so far among the eddying drifts that whitened all the atmosphere. It seemed as if the hills were giants, and were flinging monstrous handfuls of snow at one another, in their enormous sport. So thick were the fluttering snow-flakes, that even the trees, midway down the valley, were hidden by them the greater part of the time. Sometimes, it is true, the little prisoners of Tanglewood could discern a dim outline of Monument Mountain, and the smooth whiteness of the frozen lake at its base, and the black or gray tracts of woodland in the nearer landscape. But these were merely peeps through the tempest.

Nevertheless, the children rejoiced greatly in the snow-storm. They had already made acquaintance with it, by tumbling heels over head into its highest drifts, and flinging snow at one another, as we have just fancied the Berkshire mountains to be doing. And now they had come back to their spacious play-room, which was as big as the great drawing-room, and was lumbered with all sorts of playthings, large and small. The biggest was a rocking-horse, that looked like a real pony; and there was a whole family of wooden, waxen, plaster, and china dolls, besides rag-babies; and blocks enough to build Bunker Hill Monument, and nine-pins, and balls, and humming-tops, and battledores, and grace-sticks, and skipping-ropes, and more of such valuable property than I could tell of in a printed page. But the children liked the snow-storm better than them all. It suggested so many brisk enjoyments for to-morrow, and all the remainder of the winter. The sleighride; the slides down hill into the valley; the snow-images that were to be shaped out; the snow-fortresses that were to be built; and the snowballing to be carried on!

So the little folks blessed the snow-storm, and were glad to see it come thicker and thicker, and watched hopefully the long drift that was piling itself up in the avenue, and was already higher than any of their heads.

"Why, we shall be blocked up till spring!" cried they, with the hugest delight. "What a pity that the house is too high to be quite covered up! The little red house, down yonder, will be buried up to its eaves."

"You silly children, what do you want of more snow?" asked Eustace, who, tired of some novel that he was skimming through, had strolled into the play-room. "It has done mischief enough already, by spoiling the only skating that I could hope for through the winter. We shall see nothing more of the lake till April; and this was to have been my first day upon it! Don't you pity me, Primrose?"

"Oh, to be sure!" answered Primrose, laughing. "But, for your comfort, we will listen to another of your old stories, such as you told us under the porch, and down in the hollow, by Shadow Brook. Perhaps I shall like them better now, when there is nothing to do, than while there were nuts to be gathered, and beautiful weather to enjoy."

Hereupon, Periwinkle, Clover, Sweet Fern, and as many others of the little fraternity and cousinhood as were still at Tanglewood, gathered about Eustace, and earnestly besought him for a story. The student yawned, stretched himself, and then, to the vast admiration of the small people, skipped three times back and forth over the top of a chair, in order, as he explained to them, to set his wits in motion.

"Well, well, children," said he, after these preliminaries, "since you insist, and Primrose has set her heart upon it, I will see what can be done for you. And, that you may know what happy days there were before snow-storms came into fashion, I will tell you a story of the oldest of all old times, when the world was as new as Sweet Fern's bran-new humming-top. There was then but one season in the year, and that was the delightful summer; and but one age for mortals, and that was childhood."

"I never heard of that before," said Primrose.

"Of course, you never did," answered Eustace. "It shall be a story of what nobody but myself ever dreamed of,—a Paradise of children,—and how, by the naughtiness of just such a little imp as Primrose here, it all came to nothing."

So Eustace Bright sat down in the chair which he had just been skipping over, took Cowslip upon his knee, ordered silence throughout the auditory, and began a story about a sad naughty child, whose name was Pandora, and about her playfellow Epimetheus.

You may read it, word for word, in the pages that come next.

·THE·PARADISE·OF·CHILDREN·

ONG, LONG AGO, WHEN THIS OLD world was in its tender infancy, there was a child, named Epimetheus, who never had either father or mother; and, that he might not be lonely, another child, fatherless and motherless like himself, was sent from a far country, to live with him, and be his playfellow and helpmate. Her name was Pandora.

The first thing that Pandora saw, when she entered the cottage where Epimetheus dwelt, was a great box. And almost the first question which she put to him, after crossing the threshold, was this,—

"Epimetheus, what have you in that box?"

"My dear little Pandora," answered Epimetheus, "that is a secret, and you must be kind enough not to ask any questions about it. The box was left here to be kept safely, and I do not myself know what it contains."

"But who gave it to you?" asked Pandora. "And where did it come from?"

"That is a secret, too," replied Epimetheus.

"How provoking!" exclaimed Pandora, pouting her lip. "I wish the great ugly box were out of the way!"

"Oh come, don't think of it any more," cried Epimetheus. "Let us run out of doors, and have some nice play with the other children."

It is thousands of years since Epimetheus and Pandora were alive; and the world, nowadays, is a very different sort of thing from what it was in their time. Then, everybody was a child. There needed no fathers and mothers to take care of the children; because there was no danger, nor trouble of any kind, and no clothes to be mended, and there was always plenty to eat and drink. Whenever a child wanted his dinner, he found it growing on a tree; and, if he looked at the tree in the morning, he could see the expanding blossom of that night's supper; or, at eventide, he saw the tender bud of to-morrow's breakfast. It was a very pleasant life indeed. No labor to be done, no tasks to be studied; nothing but sports and dances, and sweet voices of children talking, or carolling like birds, or gushing out in merry laughter, throughout the livelong day.

What was most wonderful of all, the children never quarreled among themselves; neither had they any crying fits; nor, since time first began, had a single one of these little mortals ever gone apart into a corner, and sulked. Oh, what a good time was that to be alive in! The truth is, those ugly little winged monsters, called Troubles, which are now almost as numerous as mosquitoes, had never yet been seen on the earth. It is probable that the very greatest disquietude which a child had ever experienced was Pandora's vexation at not being able to discover the secret of the mysterious box.

This was at first only the faint shadow of a Trouble; but, every day, it grew more and more substantial, until, before a great while, the cottage of Epimetheus and Pandora was less sunshiny than those of the other children.

"Whence can the box have come?" Pandora continually kept saying to herself and to Epimetheus. "And what in the world can be inside of it?"

"Always talking about this box!" said Epimetheus, at last; for he had grown extremely tired of the subject. "I wish, dear Pandora, you would try to talk of something else. Come, let us go and gather some ripe figs, and eat them under the trees, for our supper. And I know a vine that has the sweetest and juiciest grapes you ever tasted."

"Always talking about grapes and figs!" cried Pandora, pettishly.

"Well, then," said Epimetheus, who was a very good-tempered child, like a multitude of children in those days, "let us run out and have a merry time with our playmates."

"I am tired of merry times, and don't care if I never have any more!" answered our pettish little Pandora. "And, besides, I never do have any. This ugly box! I am so taken up with thinking about it all the time. I insist upon your telling me what is inside of it."

"As I have already said, fifty times over, I do not know!" replied Epimetheus, getting a little vexed. "How, then, can I tell you what is inside?"

"You might open it," said Pandora, looking sideways at Epimetheus, "and then we could see for ourselves."

"Pandora, what are you thinking of?" exclaimed Epimetheus.

PLATE 9
Pandora wonders at the box

And his face expressed so much horror at the idea of looking into a box, which had been confided to him on the condition of his never opening it, that Pandora thought it best not to suggest it any more. Still, however, she could not help thinking and talking about the box.

"At least," said she, "you can tell me how it came here."

"It was just left at the door," replied Epimetheus, "just before you came, by a person who looked very smiling and intelligent, and who could hardly forbear laughing as he put it down. He was dressed in an odd kind of a cloak, and had on a cap that seemed to be made partly of feathers, so that it looked almost as if it had wings."

"What sort of a staff had he?" asked Pandora.

"Oh, the most curious staff you ever saw!" cried Epimetheus. "It was like two serpents twisting around a stick, and was carved so naturally that I, at first, thought the serpents were alive."

"I know him," said Pandora, thoughtfully. "Nobody else has such a staff. It was Quicksilver; and he brought me hither, as well as the box. No doubt he intended it for me; and, most probably, it contains pretty dresses for me to wear, or toys for you and me to play with, or something very nice for us both to eat!"

"Perhaps so," answered Epimetheus, turning away. "But until Quicksilver comes back and tells us so, we have neither of us any right to lift the lid of the box."

"What a dull boy he is!" muttered Pandora, as Epimetheus left the cottage. "I do wish he had a little more enterprise!"

For the first time since her arrival, Epimetheus had gone out without asking Pandora to accompany him. He went to gather figs and grapes by himself, or to seek whatever amusement he could find, in other society than his little playfellow's. He was tired to death of hearing about the box, and heartily wished that Quicksilver, or whatever was the messenger's name, had left it at some other child's door, where Pandora would never have set eyes on it. So perseveringly as she did babble about this one thing! The box, the box, and nothing but the box! It seemed as if the box were bewitched, and as if the cottage were not big enough to hold it, without Pandora's continually stumbling over it, and making Epimetheus stumble over it likewise, and bruising all four of their shins.

Well, it was really hard that poor Epimetheus should have a box in his ears from morning till night; especially as the little people of the earth were so unaccustomed to vexations, in those happy days, that they knew not how to deal with them. Thus, a small vexation made as much disturbance then, as a far bigger one would in our own times.

After Epimetheus was gone, Pandora stood gazing at the box. She had called it ugly, above a hundred times; but, in spite of all that she had said against it, it was positively a very handsome article of furniture, and would have been quite an ornament to any room in which it should be placed. It was made of a beautiful kind of wood, with dark and rich veins spreading over its surface, which was so highly polished that little Pandora could see her face in it. As the child had no other looking-glass, it is odd that she did not value the box, merely on this account.

The edges and corners of the box were carved with most wonderful skill. Around the margin there were figures of graceful men and women, and the prettiest children ever seen, reclining or sporting amid a profusion of flowers and foliage; and these various objects were so exquisitely represented, and were wrought together in such harmony, that flowers, foliage, and human beings seemed to combine into a wreath of mingled beauty. But here and there, peeping forth from behind the carved foliage, Pandora once or twice fancied that she saw a face not so lovely, or something or other that was disagreeable, and which stole the beauty out of all the rest. Nevertheless, on looking more closely, and touching the spot with her finger, she could discover nothing of the kind. Some face, that was really beautiful, had been made to look ugly by her catching a sideway glimpse at it.

The most beautiful face of all was done in what is called high relief, in the centre of the lid. There was nothing else, save the dark, smooth richness of the polished wood, and this one face in the centre, with a garland of flowers about its brow. Pandora had looked at this face a great many times, and imagined that the mouth could smile if it liked, or be grave when it chose, the same as any living mouth. The features, indeed, all wore a very lively and rather mischievous expression, which looked almost as if it needs must burst out of the carved lips, and utter itself in words.

Had the mouth spoken, it would probably have been something like this:—

"Do not be afraid, Pandora! What harm can there be in opening the box? Never mind that poor, simple Epimetheus! You are wiser than he, and have ten times as much spirit. Open the box, and see if you do not find something very pretty!"

The box, I had almost forgotten to say, was fastened; not by a lock, nor by any other such contrivance, but by a very intricate knot of gold cord. There appeared to be no end to this knot, and no beginning. Never was a knot so cunningly twisted, nor with so many ins and outs, which roguishly defied the skillfullest fingers to disentangle them. And yet, by the very difficulty that there was in it, Pandora was the more tempted to examine the knot, and just see how it was made. Two or three times, already, she had stooped over the box, and taken the knot between her thumb. and forefinger, but without positively trying to undo it.

"I really believe," said she to herself, "that I begin to see how it was done. Nay, perhaps I could tie it up again, after undoing it. There would be no harm in that, surely. Even Epimetheus would not blame me for that. I need not open the box, and should not, of course, without the foolish boy's consent, even if the knot were untied."

It might have been better for Pandora if she had had a little work to do, or anything to employ her mind upon, so as not to be so constantly thinking of this one subject. But children led so easy a life, before any Troubles came into the world, that they had really a great deal too much leisure. They could not be forever playing at hide-and-seek among the flower-shrubs, or at blind-man's-buff with garlands over their eyes, or at whatever other games had been found out, while Mother Earth was in her babyhood. When life is all sport, toil is the real play. There was absolutely nothing to do. A little sweeping and dusting about the cottage, I suppose, and the gathering of fresh flowers (which were only too abundant everywhere), and arranging them in vases,— and poor little Pandora's day's work was over. And then, for the rest of the day, there was the box!

After all, I am not quite sure that the box was not a blessing to her in its way. It supplied her with such a variety of ideas to think of, and to talk about, whenever she had anybody to listen! When she was in good-humor, she could admire the bright polish of its sides, and the rich border of beautiful faces and foliage that ran all around it. Or, if she chanced to be ill-tempered, she could give it a push, or kick it with her naughty little foot. And many a kick did the box—(but it was a mischievous box, as we shall see, and deserved all it got)—many a kick did it receive. But, certain it is, if it had not been for the box, our active-minded little Pandora would not have known half so well how to spend her time as she now did.

For it was really an endless employment to guess what was inside. What could it be, indeed? Just imagine, my little hearers, how busy your wits would be, if there were a great box in the house, which, as you might have reason to suppose, contained something new and pretty for your Christmas or New Year's gifts. Do you think that you should be less curious than Pandora? If you were left alone with the box, might you not feel a little tempted to lift the lid? But you would not do it. Oh, fie! No, no! Only, if you thought there were toys in it, it would be so very hard to let slip an opportunity of taking just one peep! I know not whether Pandora expected any toys; for none had yet begun to be made, probably, in those days, when the world itself was one great plaything for the children that dwelt upon it. But Pandora was convinced that there was something very beautiful and valuable in the box; and therefore she felt just as anxious to take a peep as any of these little girls, here around me, would have felt. And, possibly, a little more so; but of that I am not quite so certain.

On this particular day, however, which we have so long been talking about, her curiosity grew so much greater than it usually was, that, at last, she approached the box. She was more than half determined to open it, if she could. Ah, naughty Pandora!

PLATE 10
Pandora desires to open the box

First, however, she tried to lift it. It was heavy; quite too heavy for the slender strength of a child, like Pandora. She raised one end of the box a few inches from the floor, and let it fall again, with a pretty loud thump. A moment afterwards, she almost fancied that she heard something stir inside of the box. She applied her ear as closely as possible, and listened. Positively, there did seem to be a kind of stifled murmur, within! Or was it merely the singing in Pandora's ears? Or could it be the beating of her heart? The child could not quite satisfy herself whether she had heard anything or no. But, at all events, her curiosity was stronger than ever.

As she drew back her head, her eyes fell upon the knot of gold cord.

"It must have been a very ingenious person who tied this knot," said Pandora to herself. "But I think I could untie it nevertheless. I am resolved, at least, to find the two ends of the cord."

So she took the golden knot in her fingers, and pried into its intricacies as sharply as she could. Almost without intending it, or quite knowing what she was about, she was soon busily engaged in attempting to undo it. Meanwhile, the bright sunshine came through the open window; as did likewise the merry voices of the children, playing at a distance, and perhaps the voice of Epimetheus among them. Pandora stopped to listen. What a beautiful day it was! Would it not be wiser, if she were to let the troublesome knot alone, and think no more about the box, but run and join her little playfellows, and be happy?

All this time, however, her fingers were half unconsciously busy with the knot; and happening to glance at the flower-wreathed face on the lid of the enchanted box, she seemed to perceive it slyly grinning at her.

"That face looks very mischievous," thought Pandora. "I wonder whether it smiles because I am doing wrong! I have the greatest mind in the world to run away!"

But just then, by the merest accident, she gave the knot a kind of a twist, which produced a wonderful result. The gold cord untwined itself, as if by magic, and left the box without a fastening.

"This is the strangest thing I ever knew!" said Pandora. "What will Epimetheus say? And how can I possibly tie it up again?"

She made one or two attempts to restore the knot, but soon found it quite beyond her skill. It had disentangled itself so suddenly that she could not in the least remember how the strings had been doubled into one another; and when she tried to recollect the shape and appearance of the knot, it seemed to have gone entirely out of her mind. Nothing was to be done, therefore, but to let the box remain as it was until Epimetheus should come in.

"But," said Pandora, "when he finds the knot untied, he will know that I have done it. How shall I make him believe that I have not looked into the box?"

And then the thought came into her naughty little heart, that, since she would be suspected of having looked into the box, she might just as well do so at once. Oh, very naughty and very foolish Pandora! You should have thought only of doing what was right, and of leaving undone what was wrong, and not of what your playfellow Epimetheus would have said or believed. And so perhaps she might, if the enchanted face on the lid of the box had not looked so bewitchingly persuasive at her, and if she had not seemed to hear, more distinctly than before, the murmur of small voices within. She could not tell whether it was fancy or no; but there was quite a little tumult of whispers in her ear,—or else it was her curiosity that whispered,—

"Let us out, dear Pandora,—pray let us out! We will be such nice pretty playfellows for you! Only let us out!"

"What can it be?" thought Pandora. "Is there something alive in the box? Well!—yes!—I am resolved to take just one peep! Only one peep; and then the lid shall be shut down as safely as ever! There cannot possibly be any harm in just one little peep!"

But it is now time for us to see what Epimetheus was doing.

This was the first time, since his little playmate had come to dwell with him, that he had attempted to enjoy any pleasure in which she did not partake. But nothing went right; nor was he nearly so happy as on other days. He could not find a sweet grape or a ripe fig (if Epimetheus had a fault, it was a little too much fondness for figs); or, if ripe at all, they were over-ripe, and so sweet as to be cloying. There was no mirth in his heart, such as usually made his voice gush out, of its own accord, and swell the merriment of his companions. In short, he grew so uneasy and discontented, that the other children could not imagine what was the matter with Epimetheus. Neither did he himself know what ailed him, any better than they did. For you must recollect that, at the time we are speaking of, it was everybody's nature, and constant habit, to be happy. The world had not yet learned to be otherwise. Not a single soul or body, since these children were first sent to enjoy themselves on the beautiful earth, had ever been sick or out of sorts.

At length, discovering that, somehow or other, he put a stop to all the play, Epimetheus judged it best to go back to Pandora, who was in a humor better suited to his own. But, with a hope of giving her pleasure, he gathered some flowers, and made them into a wreath, which he meant to put upon her head. The flowers were very lovely,—roses, and lilies, and orange-blossoms, and a great many more, which left a trail of fragrance behind, as Epimetheus carried them along; and the wreath was put together with as much skill as could reasonably be expected of a boy. The fingers of little girls, it has always appeared to me, are the fittest to twine flower-wreaths; but boys could do it, in those days, rather better than they can now.

And here I must mention that a great black cloud had been gathering in the sky, for some time past, although it had not yet overspread the sun. But, just as Epimetheus reached the cottage door, this cloud began to intercept the sunshine, and thus to make a sudden and sad obscurity.

He entered softly; for he meant, if possible, to steal behind Pandora, and fling the wreath of flowers over her head, before she should be aware of his approach. But, as it happened, there was no need of his treading so very lightly. He might have trod as heavily as he pleased,—as heavily as a grown man,—as heavily, I was going to say, as an elephant,—without much probability of Pandora's hearing his footsteps. She was too intent upon her purpose. At the moment of his entering the cottage, the naughty child had put her hand to the lid, and was on the point of opening the mysterious box. Epimetheus beheld her. If he had cried out, Pandora would probably have withdrawn her hand, and the fatal mystery of the box might never have been known.

But Epimetheus himself, although he said very little about it, had his own share of curiosity to know what was inside. Perceiving that Pandora was resolved to find out the secret, he determined that his playfellow should not be the only wise person in the cottage. And if there were anything pretty or valuable in the box, he meant to take half of it to himself. Thus, after all his sage speeches to Pandora about restraining her curiosity, Epimetheus turned out to be quite as foolish, and nearly as much in fault, as she. So, whenever we blame Pandora for what happened, we must not forget to shake our heads at Epimetheus likewise.

As Pandora raised the lid, the cottage grew very dark and dismal; for the black cloud had now swept quite over the sun, and seemed to have buried it alive. There had, for a little while past, been a low growling and muttering, which all at once broke into a heavy peal of thunder. But Pandora, heeding nothing of all this, lifted the lid nearly upright, and looked inside. It seemed as if a sudden swarm of winged creatures brushed past her, taking flight out of the box, while, at the same instant, she heard the voice of Epimetheus, with a lamentable tone, as if he were in pain.

"Oh, I am stung!" cried he. "I am stung! Naughty Pandora! why have you opened this wicked box?"

Pandora let fall the lid, and, starting up, looked about her, to see what had befallen Epimetheus. The thunder-cloud had so darkened the room that she could not very clearly discern what was in it. But she heard a disagreeable buzzing, as if a great many huge flies, or gigantic mosquitoes, or those insects which we call dor-bugs, and pinching-dogs, were darting about. And, as her eyes grew more accustomed to the imperfect light, she saw a crowd of ugly little shapes, with bats' wings, looking abominably spiteful, and armed with terribly long stings in their tails. It was one of these that had stung Epimetheus. Nor was it a great while before Pandora herself began to scream, in no less pain and affright than her playfellow,

PLATE 11
Pandora opens the box

and making a vast deal more hubbub about it. An odious little monster had settled on her forehead, and would have stung her I know
not how deeply, if Epimetheus had not run and brushed it away.

Now, if you wish to know what these ugly things might be,
which had made their escape out of the box, I must tell you that
they were the whole family of earthly Troubles. There were evil
Passions; there were a great many species of Cares; there were
more than a hundred and fifty Sorrows; there were Diseases, in
a vast number of miserable and painful shapes; there were more
kinds of Naughtiness than it would be of any use to talk about.
In short, everything that has since afflicted the souls and bodies
of mankind had been shut up in the mysterious box, and given to
Epimetheus and Pandora to be kept safely, in order that the happy
children of the world might never be molested by them. Had they
been faithful to their trust, all would have gone well. No grown
person would ever have been sad, nor any child have had cause to
shed a single tear, from that hour until this moment.

But—and you may see by this how a wrong act of any one
mortal is a calamity to the whole world—by Pandora's lifting the
lid of that miserable box, and by the fault of Epimetheus, too, in
not preventing her, these Troubles have obtained a foothold among
us, and do not seem very likely to be driven away in a hurry. For
it was impossible, as you will easily guess, that the two children
should keep the ugly swarm in their own little cottage. On the
contrary, the first thing that they did was to fling open the doors
and windows, in hopes of getting rid of them; and, sure enough,
away flew the winged Troubles all abroad, and so pestered and
tormented the small people, everywhere about, that none of them
so much as smiled for many days afterwards. And, what was very

singular, all the flowers and dewy blossoms on earth, not one of which had hitherto faded, now began to droop and shed their leaves, after a day or two. The children, moreover, who before seemed immortal in their childhood, now grew older, day by day, and came soon to be youths and maidens, and men and women by and by, and aged people, before they dreamed of such a thing.

Meanwhile, the naughty Pandora, and hardly less naughty Epimetheus, remained in their cottage. Both of them had been grievously stung, and were in a good deal of pain, which seemed the more intolerable to them, because it was the very first pain that had ever been felt since the world began. Of course, they were entirely unaccustomed to it, and could have no idea what it meant. Besides all this, they were in exceedingly bad humor, both with themselves and with one another. In order to indulge it to the utmost, Epimetheus sat down sullenly in a corner with his back towards Pandora; while Pandora flung herself upon the floor and rested her head on the fatal and abominable box. She was crying bitterly, and sobbing as if her heart would break.

Suddenly there was a gentle little tap on the inside of the lid.

"What can that be?" cried Pandora, lifting her head.

But either Epimetheus had not heard the tap, or was too much out of humor to notice it. At any rate, he made no answer.

"You are very unkind," said Pandora, sobbing anew, "not to speak to me!"

Again the tap! It sounded like the tiny knuckles of a fairy's hand, knocking lightly and playfully on the inside of the box.

"Who are you?" asked Pandora, with a little of her former curiosity. "Who are you, inside of this naughty box?"

A sweet little voice spoke from within,—

"Only lift the lid, and you shall see."

"No, no," answered Pandora, again beginning to sob, "I have had enough of lifting the lid! You are inside of the box, naughty creature, and there you shall stay! There are plenty of your ugly brothers and sisters already flying about the world. You need never think that I shall be so foolish as to let you out!"

She looked towards Epimetheus, as she spoke, perhaps expecting that he would commend her for her wisdom. But the sullen boy only muttered that she was wise a little too late.

"Ah," said the sweet little voice again, "you had much better let me out. I am not like those naughty creatures that have stings in their tails. They are no brothers and sisters of mine, as you would see at once, if you were only to get a glimpse of me. Come, come, my pretty Pandora! I am sure you will let me out!"

And, indeed, there was a kind of cheerful witchery in the tone, that made it almost impossible to refuse anything which this little voice asked. Pandora's heart had insensibly grown lighter at every word that came from within the box. Epimetheus, too, though still in the corner, had turned half round, and seemed to be in rather better spirits than before.

"My dear Epimetheus," cried Pandora, "have you heard this little voice?"

"Yes, to be sure I have," answered he, but in no very good humor as yet. "And what of it?"

"Shall I lift the lid again?" asked Pandora.

"Just as you please," said Epimetheus. "You have done so much mischief already, that perhaps you may as well do a little more. One other Trouble, in such a swarm as you have set adrift about the world, can make no very great difference."

"You might speak a little more kindly!" murmured Pandora, wiping her eyes.

"Ah, naughty boy!" cried the little voice within the box, in an arch and laughing tone. "He knows he is longing to see me. Come, my dear Pandora, lift up the lid. I am in a great hurry to comfort you. Only let me have some fresh air, and you shall soon see that matters are not quite so dismal as you think them!"

"Epimetheus," exclaimed Pandora, "come what may, I am resolved to open the box!"

"And as the lid seems very heavy," cried Epimetheus, running across the room, "I will help you!"

So, with one consent, the two children again lifted the lid. Out flew a sunny and smiling little personage, and hovered about the room, throwing a light wherever she went. Have you never made the sunshine dance into dark corners, by reflecting it from a bit of looking-glass? Well, so looked the winged cheerfulness of this fairy-like stranger, amid the gloom of the cottage. She flew to Epimetheus, and laid the least touch of her finger on the inflamed spot where the Trouble had stung him, and immediately the anguish of it was gone. Then she kissed Pandora on the forehead, and her hurt was cured likewise.

After performing these good offices, the bright stranger fluttered sportively over the children's heads, and looked so sweetly at them, that they both began to think it not so very much amiss to have opened the box, since, otherwise, their cheery guest must have been kept a prisoner among those naughty imps with stings in their tails.

"Pray, who are you, beautiful creature?" inquired Pandora.

"I am to be called Hope!" answered the sunshiny figure. "And because I am such a cheery little body, I was packed into the box, to make amends to the human race for that swarm of ugly Troubles, which was destined to be let loose among them. Never fear! we shall do pretty well in spite of them all."

"Your wings are colored like the rainbow!" exclaimed Pandora. "How very beautiful!"

"Yes, they are like the rainbow," said Hope, "because, glad as my nature is, I am partly made of tears as well as smiles."

"And will you stay with us," asked Epimetheus, "forever and ever?"

"As long as you need me," said Hope, with her pleasant smile,—"and that will be as long as you live in the world,— I promise never to desert you. There may come times and seasons, now and then, when you will think that I have utterly vanished. But again, and again, and again, when perhaps you least dream of it, you shall see the glimmer of my wings on the ceiling of your cottage. Yes, my dear children, and I know something very good and beautiful that is to be given you hereafter!"

"Oh, tell us," they exclaimed,—"tell us what it is!"

"Do not ask me," replied Hope, putting her finger on her rosy mouth. "But do not despair, even if it should never happen while you live on this earth. Trust in my promise, for it is true."

"We do trust you!" cried Epimetheus and Pandora, both in one breath.

And so they did; and not only they, but so has everybody trusted Hope, that has since been alive. And to tell you the truth, I cannot help being glad—(though, to be sure, it was an uncommonly naughty thing for her to do)—but I cannot help being glad that our foolish Pandora peeped into the box. No doubt—no doubt—the Troubles are still flying about the world, and have increased in multitude, rather than lessened, and are a very ugly set of imps, and carry most venomous stings in their tails. I have felt them already, and expect to feel them more, as I grow older. But then that lovely and lightsome little figure of Hope! What in the world could we do without her? Hope spiritualizes the earth; Hope makes it always new; and, even in the earth's best and brightest aspect, Hope shows it to be only the shadow of an infinite bliss hereafter.

TANGLEWOOD PLAY ROOM

AFTER THE STORY

RIMROSE," ASKED EUSTACE, PINCHING her ear, "how do you like my little Pandora? Don't you think her the exact picture of yourself? But you would not have hesitated half so long about opening the box."

"Then I should have been well punished for my naughtiness," retorted Primrose, smartly; "for the first thing to pop out, after the lid was lifted, would have been Mr. Eustace Bright, in the shape of a Trouble."

"Cousin Eustace," said Sweet Fern, "did the box hold all the trouble that has ever come into the world?"

"Every mite of it!" answered Eustace. "This very snow-storm, which has spoiled my skating, was packed up there."

"And how big was the box?" asked Sweet Fern.

"Why, perhaps three feet long," said Eustace, "two feet wide, and two feet and a half high."

"Ah," said the child, "you are making fun of me, Cousin Eustace! I know there is not trouble enough in the world to fill such a great box as that. As for the snow-storm, it is no trouble at all, but a pleasure; so it could not have been in the box."

"Hear the child!" cried Primrose, with an air of superiority. "How little he knows about the troubles of this world! Poor fellow! He will be wiser when he has seen as much of life as I have."

So saying, she began to skip the rope.

Meantime, the day was drawing towards its close. Out of doors the scene certainly looked dreary. There was a gray drift, far and wide, through the gathering twilight; the earth was as pathless as the air; and the bank of snow over the steps of the porch proved that nobody had entered or gone out for a good many hours past. Had there been only one child at the window of Tanglewood, gazing at this wintry prospect, it would perhaps have made him sad. But half a dozen children together, though they cannot quite turn the world into a paradise, may defy old Winter and all his storms to put them out of spirits. Eustace Bright, moreover, on the spur of the moment, invented several new kinds of play, which kept them all in a roar of merriment till bedtime, and served for the next stormy day besides.

HE SNOW-STORM LASTED ANOTHER DAY;
but what became of it afterwards, I can-
not possibly imagine. At any rate, it
entirely cleared away during the night;
and when the sun arose the next morning, it shone brightly down on as bleak
a tract of hill-country here in Berkshire, as could be seen anywhere
in the world. The frost-work had so covered the window-panes
that it was hardly possible to get a glimpse at the scenery out-
side. But, while waiting for breakfast, the small populace of
Tanglewood had scratched peep-holes with their finger-nails, and
saw with vast delight that—unless it were one or two bare patches
on a precipitous hill-side, or the gray effect of the snow, intermingled with the black pine forest—all nature was as white as a
sheet. How exceedingly pleasant! And, to make it all the better,
it was cold enough to nip one's nose short off! If people have but
life enough in them to bear it, there is nothing that so raises the
spirits, and makes the blood ripple and dance so nimbly, like a
brook down the slope of a hill, as a bright, hard frost.

No sooner was breakfast over, than the whole party, well muffled in furs and woolens, floundered forth into the midst of the snow. Well, what a day of frosty sport was this! They slid down hill into the valley, a hundred times, nobody knows how far; and, to make it all the merrier, upsetting their sledges, and tumbling head over heels, quite as often as they came safely to the bottom. And, once, Eustace Bright took Periwinkle, Sweet Fern, and Squash-Blossom, on the sledge with him, by way of insuring a safe passage; and down they went, full speed. But, behold, halfway down, the sledge hit against a hidden stump, and flung all four of its passengers into a heap; and, on gathering themselves up, there was no little Squash-Blossom to be found! Why, what could have become of the child? And while they were wondering and staring about, up started Squash-Blossom out of a snow-bank, with the reddest face you ever saw, and looking as if a large scarlet flower had suddenly sprouted up in midwinter. Then there was a great laugh.

When they had grown tired of sliding down hill, Eustace set the children to digging a cave in the biggest snow-drift that they could find. Unluckily, just as it was completed, and the party had squeezed themselves into the hollow, down came the roof upon their heads, and buried every soul of them alive! The next moment, up popped all their little heads out of the ruins, and the tall student's head in the midst of them, looking hoary and venerable with the snow-dust that had got amongst his brown curls. And then, to punish Cousin Eustace for advising them to dig such a tumble-down cavern, the children attacked him in a body, and so bepelted him with snowballs that he was fain to take to his heels.

So he ran away, and went into the woods, and thence to the margin of Shadow Brook, where he could hear the streamlet grumbling along, under great overhanging banks of snow and ice, which would scarcely let it see the light of day. There were adamantine icicles glittering around all its little cascades. Thence he strolled to the shore of the lake, and beheld a white, untrodden plain before him, stretching from his own feet to the foot of Monument Mountain. And, it being now almost sunset, Eustace thought that he had never beheld anything so fresh and beautiful as the scene. He was glad that the children were not with him; for their lively spirits and tumble-about activity would quite have chased away his higher and graver mood, so that he would merely have been merry (as he had already been, the whole day long), and would not have known the loveliness of the winter sunset among the hills.

When the sun was fairly down, our friend Eustace went home to eat his supper. After the meal was over, he betook himself to the study with a purpose, I rather imagine, to write an ode, or two or three sonnets, or verses of some kind or other, in praise of the purple and golden clouds which he had seen around the setting sun. But, before he had hammered out the very first rhyme, the door opened, and Primrose and Periwinkle made their appearance.

"Go away, children! I can't be troubled with you now!" cried the student, looking over his shoulder, with the pen between his fingers. "What in the world do you want here? I thought you were all in bed!"

"Hear him, Periwinkle, trying to talk like a grown man!" said Primrose. "And he seems to forget that I am now thirteen years old, and may sit up almost as late as I please. But, Cousin Eustace, you must put off your airs, and come with us to the drawing-room. The children have talked so much about your stories, that my father wishes to hear one of them, in order to judge whether they are likely to do any mischief."

"Poh, poh, Primrose!" exclaimed the student, rather vexed. "I don't believe I can tell one of my stories in the presence of grown people. Besides, your father is a classical scholar; not that I am much afraid of his scholarship, neither, for I doubt not it is as rusty as an old case-knife by this time. But then he will be sure to quarrel with the admirable nonsense that I put into these stories, out of my own head, and which makes the great charm of the matter for children, like yourself. No man of fifty, who has read the classical myths in his youth, can possibly understand my merit as a reinventor and improver of them."

"All this may be very true," said Primrose, "but come you must! My father will not open his book, nor will mamma open the piano, till you have given us some of your nonsense, as you very correctly call it. So be a good boy, and come along."

Whatever he might pretend, the student was rather glad than otherwise, on second thoughts, to catch at the opportunity of proving to Mr. Pringle what an excellent faculty he had in modernizing the myths of ancient times. Until twenty years of age, a young man may, indeed, be rather bashful about showing his poetry and his prose; but, for all that, he is pretty apt to think that these very productions would place him at the tiptop of literature, if once they could be known. Accordingly, without much more resistance, Eustace suffered Primrose and Periwinkle to drag him into the drawing-room.

It was a large, handsome apartment, with a semi-circular window at one end, in the recess of which stood a marble copy of

Greenough's Angel and Child. On one side of the fireplace there were many shelves of books, gravely but richly bound. The white light of the astral-lamp, and the red glow of the bright coal-fire, made the room brilliant and cheerful; and before the fire, in a deep arm-chair, sat Mr. Pringle, looking just fit to be seated in such a chair, and in such a room. He was a tall and quite a handsome gentleman, with a bald brow; and was always so nicely dressed, that even Eustace Bright never liked to enter his presence without at least pausing at the threshold to settle his shirt-collar. But now, as Primrose had hold of one of his hands, and Periwinkle of the other, he was forced to make his appearance with a rough-and-tumble sort of look, as if he had been rolling all day in a snow-bank. And so he had.

Mr. Pringle turned towards the student benignly enough, but in a way that made him feel how uncombed and unbrushed he was, and how uncombed and unbrushed, likewise, were his mind and thoughts.

"Eustace," said Mr. Pringle, with a smile, "I find that you are producing a great sensation among the little public of Tanglewood, by the exercise of your gifts of narrative. Primrose here, as the little folks choose to call her, and the rest of the children, have been so loud in praise of your stories, that Mrs. Pringle and myself are really curious to hear a specimen. It would be so much the more gratifying to myself, as the stories appear to be an attempt to render the fables of classical antiquity into the idiom of modern fancy and feeling. At least, so I judge from a few of the incidents which have come to me at second hand."

"You are not exactly the auditor that I should have chosen, sir," observed the student, "for fantasies of this nature."

"Possibly not," replied Mr. Pringle. "I suspect, however, that a young author's most useful critic is precisely the one whom he would be least apt to choose. Pray oblige me, therefore."

"Sympathy, methinks, should have some little share in the critic's qualifications," murmured Eustace Bright. "However, sir, if you will find patience, I will find stories. But be kind enough to remember that I am addressing myself to the imagination and sympathies of the children, not to your own."

Accordingly, the student snatched hold of the first theme which presented itself. It was suggested by a plate of apples that he happened to spy on the mantel-piece.

·THE·THREE·GOLDEN·APPLES·

ID YOU EVER HEAR OF THE GOLDEN apples, that grew in the garden of the Hesperides? Ah, those were such apples as would bring a great price, by the bushel, if any of them could be found growing in the orchards of nowadays! But there is not, I suppose, a graft of that wonderful fruit on a single tree in the wide world. Not so much as a seed of those apples exists any longer.

And, even in the old, old, half-forgotten times, before the garden of the Hesperides was overrun with weeds, a great many people doubted whether there could be real trees that bore apples of solid gold upon their branches. All had heard of them, but nobody remembered to have seen any. Children, nevertheless, used to listen, open-mouthed, to stories of the golden apple-tree, and resolved to discover it, when they should be big enough. Adventurous young men, who desired to do a braver thing than any of their fellows, set out in quest of this fruit. Many of them returned no more; none of them brought back the apples. No wonder that they found it impossible to gather them! It is said that there was a dragon beneath the tree, with a hundred terrible heads, fifty of which were always on the watch, while the other fifty slept.

In my opinion it was hardly worth running so much risk for the sake of a solid golden apple. Had the apples been sweet, mellow, and juicy, indeed that would be another matter. There might then have been some sense in trying to get at them, in spite of the hundred-headed dragon.

But, as I have already told you, it was quite a common thing with young persons, when tired of too much peace and rest, to go in search of the garden of the Hesperides. And once the adventure was undertaken by a hero who had enjoyed very little peace or rest since he came into the world. At the time of which I am going to speak, he was wandering through the pleasant land of Italy, with a mighty club in his hand, and a bow and quiver slung across his shoulders. He was wrapt in the skin of the biggest and fiercest lion that ever had been seen, and which he himself had killed; and though, on the whole, he was kind, and generous, and noble, there was a good deal of the lion's fierceness in his heart. As he went on his way, he continually inquired whether that were the right road to the famous garden. But none of the country people knew anything about the matter, and many looked as if they would have laughed at the question, if the stranger had not carried so very big a club.

So he journeyed on and on, still making the same inquiry, until, at last, he came to the brink of a river where some beautiful young women sat twining wreaths of flowers.

"Can you tell me, pretty maidens," asked the stranger, "whether this is the right way to the garden of the Hesperides?"

The young women had been having a fine time together, weaving the flowers into wreaths, and crowning one another's heads. And there seemed to be a kind of magic in the touch of their fingers, that made the flowers more fresh and dewy, and of brighter hues, and sweeter fragrance, while they played with them, than even when they had been growing on their native stems. But, on hearing the stranger's question, they dropped all their flowers on the grass, and gazed at him with astonishment.

"The garden of the Hesperides!" cried one. "We thought mortals had been weary of seeking it, after so many disappointments. And pray, adventurous traveler, what do you want there?"

"A certain king, who is my cousin," replied he, "has ordered me to get him three of the golden apples."

"Most of the young men who go in quest of these apples," observed another of the damsels, "desire to obtain them for themselves, or to present them to some fair maiden whom they love. Do you, then, love this king, your cousin, so very much?"

"Perhaps not," replied the stranger, sighing. "He has often been severe and cruel to me. But it is my destiny to obey him."

"And do you know," asked the damsel who had first spoken, "that a terrible dragon, with a hundred heads, keeps watch under the golden apple-tree?"

"I know it well," answered the stranger, calmly. "But, from my cradle upwards, it has been my business, and almost my pastime, to deal with serpents and dragons."

The young women looked at his massive club, and at the shaggy lion's skin which he wore, and likewise at his heroic limbs and figure; and they whispered to each other that the stranger appeared to be one who might reasonably expect to perform deeds far beyond the might of other men. But, then, the dragon with a hundred heads! What mortal, even if he possessed a hundred lives, could hope to escape the fangs of such a monster? So kind-hearted were the maidens, that they could not bear to see this brave and handsome traveler attempt what was so very dangerous, and devote himself, most probably, to become a meal for the dragon's hundred ravenous mouths.

"Go back," cried they all,—"go back to your own home! Your mother, beholding you safe and sound, will shed tears of joy; and what can she do more, should you win ever so great a victory? No matter for the golden apples! No matter for the king, your cruel cousin! We do not wish the dragon with the hundred heads to eat you up!"

The stranger seemed to grow impatient at these remonstrances. He carelessly lifted his mighty club, and let it fall upon a rock that lay half buried in the earth, near by. With the force of that idle blow, the great rock was shattered all to pieces. It cost the stranger no more effort to achieve this feat of a giant's strength than for one of the young maidens to touch her sister's rosy cheek with a flower.

"Do you not believe," said he, looking at the damsels with a smile, "that such a blow would have crushed one of the dragon's hundred heads?"

Then he sat down on the grass, and told them the story of his life, or as much of it as he could remember, from the day when he was first cradled in a warrior's brazen shield. While he lay there, two immense serpents came gliding over the floor, and opened their hideous jaws to devour him; and he, a baby of a few months old, had griped one of the fierce snakes in each of his little fists,

PLATE 12
Hercules and the Nymphs

and strangled them to death. When he was but a stripling, he had killed a huge lion, almost as big as the one whose vast and shaggy hide he now wore upon his shoulders. The next thing that he had done was to fight a battle with an ugly sort of monster, called a hydra, which had no less than nine heads, and exceedingly sharp teeth in every one.

"But the dragon of the Hesperides, you know," observed one of the damsels, "has a hundred heads!"

"Nevertheless," replied the stranger, "I would rather fight two such dragons than a single hydra. For, as fast as I cut off a head, two others grew in its place; and, besides, there was one of the heads that could not possibly be killed, but kept biting as fiercely as ever, long after it was cut off. So I was forced to bury it under a stone, where it is doubtless alive to this very day. But the hydra's body, and its eight other heads, will never do any further mischief."

The damsels, judging that the story was likely to last a good while, had been preparing a repast of bread and grapes, that the stranger might refresh himself in the intervals of his talk. They took pleasure in helping him to this simple food; and, now and then, one of them would put a sweet grape between her rosy lips, lest it should make him bashful to eat alone.

The traveler proceeded to tell how he had chased a very swift stag, for a twelvemonth together, without ever stopping to take breath, and had at last caught it by the antlers, and carried it home alive. And he had fought with a very odd race of people, half horses and half men, and had put them all to death, from a sense of duty, in order that their ugly figures might never be seen any more. Besides all this, he took to himself great credit for having cleaned out a stable.

"Do you call that a wonderful exploit?" asked one of the young maidens, with a smile. "Any clown in the country has done as much!"

"Had it been an ordinary stable," replied the stranger, "I should not have mentioned it. But this was so gigantic a task that it would have taken me all my life to perform it, if I had not luckily thought of turning the channel of a river through the stable-door. That did the business in a very short time!"

Seeing how earnestly his fair auditors listened, he next told them how he had shot some monstrous birds, and had caught a wild bull alive and let him go again, and had tamed a number of very wild horses, and had conquered Hippolyta, the warlike queen of the Amazons. He mentioned, likewise, that he had taken off Hippolyta's enchanted girdle, and had given it to the daughter of his cousin, the king.

"Was it the girdle of Venus," inquired the prettiest of the damsels, "which makes women beautiful?"

"No," answered the stranger. "It had formerly been the sword-belt of Mars; and it can only make the wearer valiant and courageous."

"An old sword-belt!" cried the damsel, tossing her head. "Then I should not care about having it!"

"You are right," said the stranger.

Going on with his wonderful narrative, he informed the maidens that as strange an adventure as ever happened was when he fought with Geryon, the six-legged man. This was a very odd and frightful sort of figure, as you may well believe. Any person, looking at his tracks in the sand or snow, would suppose that three sociable companions had been walking along together. On hearing his footsteps at a little distance, it was no more than reasonable to judge that several people must be coming. But it was only the strange man Geryon clattering onward, with his six legs!

Six legs, and one gigantic body! Certainly, he must have been a very queer monster to look at; and, my stars, what a waste of shoe-leather!

When the stranger had finished the story of his adventures, he looked around at the attentive faces of the maidens.

"Perhaps you may have heard of me before," said he, modestly. "My name is Hercules!"

"We had already guessed it," replied the maidens; "for your wonderful deeds are known all over the world. We do not think it strange, any longer, that you should set out in quest of the golden apples of the Hesperides. Come, sisters, let us crown the hero with flowers!"

Then they flung beautiful wreaths over his stately head and mighty shoulders, so that the lion's skin was almost entirely covered with roses. They took possession of his ponderous club, and so entwined it about with the brightest, softest, and most fragrant blossoms, that not a finger's breadth of its oaken substance could be seen. It looked all like a huge bunch of flowers. Lastly, they joined hands, and danced around him, chanting words which became poetry of their own accord, and grew into a choral song, in honor of the illustrious Hercules.

And Hercules was rejoiced, as any other hero would have been, to know that these fair young girls had heard of the valiant deeds which it had cost him so much toil and danger to achieve. But, still, he was not satisfied. He could not think that what he had already done was worthy of so much honor, while there remained any bold or difficult adventure to be undertaken.

"Dear maidens," said he, when they paused to take breath, "now that you know my name, will you not tell me how I am to reach the garden of the Hesperides?"

"Ah! must you go so soon?" they exclaimed. "You—that have performed so many wonders, and spent such a toilsome life—cannot you content yourself to repose a little while on the margin of this peaceful river?"

Hercules shook his head.

"I must depart now," said he.

"We will then give you the best directions we can," replied the damsels. "You must go to the sea-shore, and find out the Old One, and compel him to inform you where the golden apples are to be found."

"The Old One!" repeated Hercules, laughing at this odd name. "And, pray, who may the Old One be?"

"Why, the Old Man of the Sea, to be sure!" answered one of the damsels. "He has fifty daughters, whom some people call very beautiful; but we do not think it proper to be acquainted with them, because they have sea-green hair, and taper away like fishes. You must talk with this Old Man of the Sea. He is a sea-faring person, and knows all about the garden of the Hesperides; for it is situated in an island which he is often in the habit of visiting."

Hercules then asked whereabouts the Old One was most likely to be met with. When the damsels had informed him, he thanked them for all their kindness,—for the bread and grapes with which they had fed him, the lovely flowers with which they had crowned him, and the songs and dances wherewith they had done him honor,—and he thanked them, most of all, for telling him the right way,—and immediately set forth upon his journey.

But, before he was out of hearing, one of the maidens called after him.

"Keep fast hold of the Old One, when you catch him!" cried she, smiling, and lifting her finger to make the caution more impressive. "Do not be astonished at anything that may happen. Only hold him fast, and he will tell you what you wish to know."

Hercules again thanked her, and pursued his way, while the maidens resumed their pleasant labor of making flower-wreaths. They talked about the hero, long after he was gone.

"We will crown him with the loveliest of our garlands," said they, "when he returns hither with the three golden apples, after slaying the dragon with a hundred heads."

Meanwhile, Hercules traveled constantly onward, over hill and dale, and through the solitary woods. Sometimes he swung his club aloft, and splintered a mighty oak with a downright blow. His mind was so full of the giants and monsters with whom it was the business of his life to fight, that perhaps he mistook the great tree for a giant or a monster. And so eager was Hercules to achieve what he had undertaken, that he almost regretted to have spent so much time with the damsels, wasting idle breath upon the story of his adventures. But thus it always is with persons who are destined to perform great things. What they have already done seems less than nothing. What they have taken in hand to do seems worth toil, danger, and life itself.

Persons who happened to be passing through the forest must have been affrighted to see him smite the trees with his great club. With but a single blow, the trunk was riven as by the stroke of lightning, and the broad boughs came rustling and crashing down.

Hastening forward, without ever pausing or looking behind, he by and by heard the sea roaring at a distance. At this sound, he increased his speed, and soon came to a beach, where the great surf-waves tumbled themselves upon the hard sand, in a long line of snowy foam. At one end of the beach, however, there was a pleasant spot, where some green shrubbery clambered up a cliff, making its rocky face look soft and beautiful. A carpet of verdant grass, largely intermixed with sweet-smelling clover, covered the narrow space between the bottom of the cliff and the sea. And what should Hercules espy there, but an old man, fast asleep!

But was it really and truly an old man? Certainly, at first sight, it looked very like one; but, on closer inspection, it rather seemed to be some kind of a creature that lived in the sea. For, on his legs and arms there were scales, such as fishes have; he was web-footed and web-fingered, after the fashion of a duck; and his long beard, being of a greenish tinge, had more the appearance of a tuft of sea-weed than of an ordinary beard. Have you never seen a stick of timber, that has been long tossed about by the waves, and has got all overgrown with barnacles, and, at last drifting ashore, seems to have been thrown up from the very deepest bottom of the sea? Well, the old man would have put you in mind of just such a wave-tost spar! But Hercules, the instant he set eyes on this strange figure, was convinced that it could be no other than the Old One, who was to direct him on his way.

Yes, it was the selfsame Old Man of the Sea whom the hospitable maidens had talked to him about. Thanking his stars for the

PLATE 13
Hercules and the Old Man
of the Sea

lucky accident of finding the old fellow asleep, Hercules stole on tiptoe towards him, and caught him by the arm and leg.

"Tell me," cried he, before the Old One was well awake, "which is the way to the garden of the Hesperides?"

As you may easily imagine, the Old Man of the Sea awoke in a fright. But his astonishment could hardly have been greater than was that of Hercules, the next moment. For, all of a sudden, the Old One seemed to disappear out of his grasp, and he found himself holding a stag by the fore and hind leg! But still he kept fast hold. Then the stag disappeared, and in its stead there was a sea-bird, fluttering and screaming, while Hercules clutched it by the wing and claw! But the bird could not get away. Immediately afterwards, there was an ugly three-headed dog, which growled and barked at Hercules, and snapped fiercely at the hands by which he held him! But Hercules would not let him go. In another minute, instead of the three-headed dog, what should appear but Geryon, the six-legged man-monster, kicking at Hercules with five of his legs, in order to get the remaining one at liberty! But Hercules held on. By and by, no Geryon was there, but a huge snake, like one of those which Hercules had strangled in his baby-hood, only a hundred times as big; and it twisted and twined about the hero's neck and body, and threw its tail high into the air, and opened its deadly jaws as if to devour him outright; so that it was really a very terrible spectacle! But Hercules was no whit disheartened, and squeezed the great snake so tightly that he soon began to hiss with pain.

You must understand that the Old Man of the Sea, though he generally looked so much like the wave-beaten figure-head of a vessel, had the power of assuming any shape he pleased. When he found himself so roughly seized by Hercules, he had been in hopes of putting him into such surprise and terror, by these magical transformations, that the hero would be glad to let him go. If Hercules had relaxed his grasp, the Old One would certainly have plunged down to the very bottom of the sea, whence he would not soon have given himself the trouble of coming up, in order to answer any impertinent questions. Ninety-nine people out of a hundred, I suppose, would have been frightened out of their wits by the very first of his ugly shapes, and would have taken to their heels at once. For, one of the hardest things in this world is, to see the difference between real dangers and imaginary ones.

But, as Hercules held on so stubbornly, and only squeezed the Old One so much the tighter at every change of shape, and really put him to no small torture, he finally thought it best to reappear in his own figure. So there he was again, a fishy, scaly, web-footed sort of personage, with something like a tuft of sea-weed at his chin.

"Pray, what do you want with me?" cried the Old One, as soon as he could take breath; for it is quite a tiresome affair to go through so many false shapes. "Why do you squeeze me so hard? Let me go, this moment, or I shall begin to consider you an extremely uncivil person!"

"My name is Hercules!" roared the mighty stranger. "And you will never get out of my clutch, until you tell me the nearest way to the garden of the Hesperides!"

When the old fellow heard who it was that had caught him, he saw, with half an eye, that it would be necessary to tell him everything that he wanted to know. The Old One was an inhabitant of the sea, you must recollect, and roamed about everywhere, like other sea-faring people. Of course, he had often heard of the fame of Hercules, and of the wonderful things that he was constantly performing, in various parts of the earth, and how determined he always was to accomplish whatever he undertook. He therefore made no more attempts to escape, but told the hero how to find the garden of the Hesperides, and likewise warned him of many difficulties which must be overcome, before he could arrive thither.

"You must go on, thus and thus," said the Old Man of the Sea, after taking the points of the compass, "till you come in sight of a very tall giant, who holds the sky on his shoulders. And the giant, if he happens to be in the humor, will tell you exactly where the garden of the Hesperides lies."

"And if the giant happens not to be in the humor," remarked Hercules, balancing his club on the tip of his finger, "perhaps I shall find means to persuade him!"

Thanking the Old Man of the Sea, and begging his pardon for having squeezed him so roughly, the hero resumed his journey. He met with a great many strange adventures, which would be well worth your hearing, if I had leisure to narrate them as minutely as they deserve.

It was in this journey, if I mistake not, that he encountered a prodigious giant, who was so wonderfully contrived by nature, that every time he touched the earth he became ten times as strong as ever he had been before. His name was Antæus. You may see, plainly enough, that it was a very difficult business to fight with such a fellow; for, as often as he got a knock-down blow, up he started again, stronger, fiercer, and abler to use his weapons, than if his enemy had let him alone. Thus, the harder Hercules pounded the giant with his club, the further he seemed from winning the victory. I have sometimes argued with such people, but never fought with one. The only way in which Hercules found it possible to finish the battle, was by lifting Antæus off his feet into the air, and squeezing, and squeezing, and squeezing him, until, finally, the strength was quite squeezed out of his enormous body.

When this affair was finished, Hercules continued his travels, and went to the land of Egypt, where he was taken prisoner, and would have been put to death, if he had not slain the king of the country, and made his escape. Passing through the deserts of Africa, and going as fast as he could, he arrived at last on the shore of the great ocean. And here, unless he could walk on the crests of the billows, it seemed as if his journey must needs be at an end.

Nothing was before him, save the foaming, dashing, measureless ocean. But, suddenly, as he looked towards the horizon, he saw something, a great way off, which he had not seen the moment before. It gleamed very brightly, almost as you may have beheld the round, golden disk of the sun, when it rises or sets over the edge of the world. It evidently drew nearer; for, at every instant, this wonderful object became larger and more lustrous. At length, it had come so nigh that Hercules discovered it to be an immense cup or bowl, made either of gold or burnished brass. How it had got afloat upon the sea is more than I can tell you. There it was, at all events, rolling on the tumultuous billows, which tossed it up and down, and heaved their foamy tops against its sides, but without ever throwing their spray over the brim.

"I have seen many giants, in my time," thought Hercules, "but never one that would need to drink his wine out of a cup like this!"

And, true enough, what a cup it must have been! It was as large—as large—but, in short, I am afraid to say how immeasurably large it was. To speak within bounds, it was ten times larger than a great mill-wheel; and, all of metal as it was, it floated over the heaving surges more lightly than an acorn-cup adown the brook. The waves tumbled it onward, until it grazed against the shore, within a short distance of the spot where Hercules was standing.

As soon as this happened, he knew what was to be done; for he had not gone through so many remarkable adventures without learning pretty well how to conduct himself, whenever anything came to pass a little out of the common rule. It was just as clear as daylight that this marvelous cup had been set adrift by some unseen power, and guided hitherward, in order to carry Hercules across the sea, on his way to the garden of the Hesperides. Accordingly, without a moment's delay, he clambered over the brim, and slid down on the inside, where, spreading out his lion's skin, he proceeded to take a little repose. He had scarcely rested, until now, since he bade farewell to the damsels on the margin of the river. The waves dashed, with a pleasant and ringing sound, against the circumference of the hollow cup; it rocked lightly to and fro, and the motion was so soothing that it speedily rocked Hercules into an agreeable slumber.

His nap had probably lasted a good while, when the cup chanced to graze against a rock, and, in consequence, immediately resounded and reverberated through its golden or brazen substance, a hundred times as loudly as ever you heard a church-bell. The noise awoke Hercules, who instantly started up and gazed around him, wondering whereabouts he was. He was not long in discovering that the cup had floated across a great part of the sea, and was approaching the shore of what seemed to be an island. And, on that island, what do you think he saw?

No; you will never guess it, not if you were to try fifty thousand times! It positively appears to me that this was the most marvelous spectacle that had ever been seen by Hercules, in the whole course of his wonderful travels and adventures. It was a greater marvel than the hydra with nine heads, which kept growing twice as fast as they were cut off; greater than the six-legged man-monster; greater than Antæus; greater than anything that was ever beheld by anybody, before or since the days of Hercules, or than anything that remains to be beheld, by travelers in all time to come. It was a giant!

But such an intolerably big giant! A giant as tall as a mountain; so vast a giant, that the clouds rested about his midst, like a girdle, and hung like a hoary beard from his chin, and flitted before his huge eyes, so that he could neither see Hercules nor the golden cup in which he was voyaging. And, most wonderful of all, the giant held up his great hands and appeared to support the sky, which, so far as Hercules could discern through the clouds, was resting upon his head! This does really seem almost too much to believe.

Meanwhile, the bright cup continued to float onward, and finally touched the strand. Just then a breeze wafted away the clouds from before the giant's visage, and Hercules beheld it, with all its enormous features; eyes each of them as big as yonder lake, a nose a mile long, and a mouth of the same width. It was a countenance terrible from its enormity of size, but disconsolate and weary, even as you may see the faces of many people, nowadays, who are compelled to sustain burdens above their strength. What the sky was to the giant, such are the cares of earth to those who let themselves be weighed down by them. And whenever men undertake what is beyond the just measure of their abilities, they encounter precisely such a doom as had befallen this poor giant.

PLATE 14
Hercules and Atlas

Poor fellow! He had evidently stood there a long while. An ancient forest had been growing and decaying around his feet; and oak-trees, of six or seven centuries old, had sprung from the acorn, and forced themselves between his toes.

The giant now looked down from the far height of his great eyes, and, perceiving Hercules, roared out, in a voice that resembled thunder, proceeding out of the cloud that had just flitted away from his face.

"Who are you, down at my feet there? And whence do you come, in that little cup?"

"I am Hercules!" thundered back the hero, in a voice pretty nearly or quite as loud as the giant's own. "And I am seeking for the garden of the Hesperides!"

"Ho! ho! ho!" roared the giant, in a fit of immense laughter. "That is a wise adventure, truly!"

"And why not?" cried Hercules, getting a little angry at the giant's mirth. "Do you think I am afraid of the dragon with a hundred heads!"

Just at this time, while they were talking together, some black clouds gathered about the giant's middle, and burst into a tremendous storm of thunder and lightning, causing such a pother that Hercules found it impossible to distinguish a word. Only the giant's immeasurable legs were to be seen, standing up into the obscurity of the tempest; and, now and then, a momentary glimpse of his whole figure, mantled in a volume of mist. He seemed to be speaking, most of the time; but his big, deep, rough voice chimed in with the reverberations of the thunder-claps, and rolled away over the hills, like them. Thus, by talking out of season, the foolish giant expended an incalculable quantity of breath, to no purpose; for the thunder spoke quite as intelligibly as he.

At last, the storm swept over, as suddenly as it had come. And there again was the clear sky, and the weary giant holding it up, and the pleasant sunshine beaming over his vast height, and illuminating it against the background of the sullen thunder-clouds. So far above the shower had been his head, that not a hair of it was moistened by the rain-drops!

When the giant could see Hercules still standing on the seashore, he roared out to him anew.

"I am Atlas, the mightiest giant in the world! And I hold the sky upon my head!"

"So I see," answered Hercules. "But, can you show me the way to the garden of the Hesperides?"

"What do you want there?" asked the giant.

"I want three of the golden apples," shouted Hercules, "for my cousin, the king."

"There is nobody but myself," quoth the giant, "that can go to the garden of the Hesperides, and gather the golden apples. If it were not for this little business of holding up the sky, I would make half a dozen steps across the sea, and get them for you."

"You are very kind," replied Hercules. "And cannot you rest the sky upon a mountain?"

"None of them are quite high enough," said Atlas, shaking his head. "But, if you were to take your stand on the summit of that nearest one, your head would be pretty nearly on a level with mine. You seem to be a fellow of some strength. What if you should take my burden on your shoulders, while I do your errand for you?"

Hercules, as you must be careful to remember, was a remarkably strong man; and though it certainly requires a great deal of muscular power to uphold the sky, yet, if any mortal could be supposed capable of such an exploit, he was the one. Nevertheless, it seemed so difficult an undertaking, that, for the first time in his life, he hesitated.

"Is the sky very heavy?" he inquired.

"Why, not particularly so, at first," answered the giant, shrugging his shoulders. "But it gets to be a little burdensome, after a thousand years!"

"And how long a time," asked the hero, "will it take you to get the golden apples?"

"Oh, that will be done in a few moments," cried Atlas. "I shall take ten or fifteen miles at a stride, and be at the garden and back again before your shoulders begin to ache."

"Well, then," answered Hercules, "I will climb the mountain behind you there, and relieve you of your burden."

The truth is, Hercules had a kind heart of his own, and considered that he should be doing the giant a favor, by allowing him this opportunity for a ramble. And, besides, he thought that it would be still more for his own glory, if he could boast of upholding the sky, than merely to do so ordinary a thing as to conquer a dragon with a hundred heads. Accordingly, without more words, the sky was shifted from the shoulders of Atlas, and placed upon those of Hercules.

When this was safely accomplished, the first thing that the giant did was to stretch himself; and you may imagine what a prodigious spectacle he was then. Next, he slowly lifted one of his feet out of the forest that had grown up around it; then, the other.

Then, all at once, he began to caper, and leap, and dance, for joy at his freedom; flinging himself nobody knows how high into the air, and floundering down again with a shock that made the earth tremble. Then he laughed—Ho! ho! ho!—with a thunderous roar that was echoed from the mountains, far and near, as if they and the giant had been so many rejoicing brothers. When his joy had a little subsided, he stepped into the sea; ten miles at the first stride, which brought him midleg deep; and ten miles at the second, when the water came just above his knees; and ten miles more at the third, by which he was immersed nearly to his waist. This was the greatest depth of the sea.

Hercules watched the giant, as he still went onward; for it was really a wonderful sight, this immense human form, more than thirty miles off, half hidden in the ocean, but with his upper half as tall, and misty, and blue, as a distant mountain. At last the gigantic shape faded entirely out of view. And now Hercules began to consider what he should do, in case Atlas should be drowned in the sea, or if he were to be stung to death by the dragon with the hundred heads, which guarded the golden apples of the Hesperides. If any such misfortune were to happen, how could he ever get rid of the sky? And, by the by, its weight began already to be a little irksome to his head and shoulders.

"I really pity the poor giant," thought Hercules. "If it wearies me so much in ten minutes, how must it have wearied him in a thousand years!"

O my sweet little people, you have no idea what a weight there was in that same blue sky, which looks so soft and aerial above our heads! And there, too, was the bluster of the wind, and the chill and watery clouds, and the blazing sun, all taking their turns to make Hercules uncomfortable! He began to be afraid that the giant would never come back. He gazed wistfully at the world beneath him, and acknowledged to himself that it was a far happier kind of life to be a shepherd at the foot of a mountain, than to stand on its dizzy summit, and bear up the firmament with his might and main. For, of course, as you will easily understand, Hercules had an immense responsibility on his mind, as well as a weight on his head and shoulders. Why, if he did not stand perfectly still, and keep the sky immovable, the sun would perhaps be put ajar! Or, after nightfall, a great many of the stars might be loosened from their places, and shower down, like fiery rain, upon the people's heads! And how ashamed would the hero be, if, owing to his unsteadiness beneath its weight, the sky should crack, and show a great fissure quite across it!

I know not how long it was before, to his unspeakable joy, he beheld the huge shape of the giant, like a cloud, on the far-off edge of the sea. At his nearer approach, Atlas held up his hand, in which Hercules could perceive three magnificent golden apples, as big as pumpkins, all hanging from one branch.

"I am glad to see you again," shouted Hercules, when the giant was within hearing. "So you have got the golden apples?"

"Certainly, certainly," answered Atlas; "and very fair apples they are. I took the finest that grew on the tree, I assure you. Ah! it is a beautiful spot, that garden of the Hesperides. Yes; and the dragon with a hundred heads is a sight worth any man's seeing. After all, you had better have gone for the apples yourself."

"No matter," replied Hercules. "You have had a pleasant ramble, and have done the business as well as I could. I heartily thank you for your trouble. And now, as I have a long way to go, and am rather in haste,—and as the king, my cousin, is anxious to receive the golden apples,—will you be kind enough to take the sky off my shoulders again?"

"Why, as to that," said the giant, chucking the golden apples into the air twenty miles high, or thereabouts, and catching them as they came down,—"as to that, my good friend, I consider you a little unreasonable. Cannot I carry the golden apples to the king, your cousin, much quicker than you could? As his majesty is in such a hurry to get them, I promise you to take my longest strides. And, besides, I have no fancy for burdening myself with the sky, just now."

Here Hercules grew impatient, and gave a great shrug of his shoulders. It being now twilight, you might have seen two or three stars tumble out of their places. Everybody on earth looked upward in affright, thinking that the sky might be going to fall next.

"Oh, that will never do!" cried Giant Atlas, with a great roar of laughter. "I have not let fall so many stars within the last five centuries. By the time you have stood there as long as I did, you will begin to learn patience!"

"What!" shouted Hercules, very wrathfully, "do you intend to make me bear this burden forever?"

"We will see about that, one of these days," answered the giant. "At all events, you ought not to complain, if you have to bear it the next hundred years, or perhaps the next thousand. I bore it a good while longer, in spite of the back-ache. Well, then, after a thousand years, if I happen to feel in the mood, we may possibly shift about again. You are certainly a very strong man, and can never have a better opportunity to prove it. Posterity will talk of you, I warrant it!"

"Pish! a fig for its talk!" cried Hercules, with another hitch of his shoulders. "Just take the sky upon your head one instant, will you? I want to make a cushion of my lion's skin, for the weight to rest upon. It really chafes me, and will cause unnecessary inconvenience in so many centuries as I am to stand here."

"That's no more than fair, and I'll do it!" quoth the giant; for he had no unkind feeling towards Hercules, and was merely acting with a too selfish consideration of his own ease. "For just five minutes, then, I'll take back the sky. Only for five minutes, recollect! I have no idea of spending another thousand years as I spent the last. Variety is the spice of life, say I."

Ah, the thick-witted old rogue of a giant! He threw down the golden apples, and received back the sky, from the head and shoulders of Hercules, upon his own, where it rightly belonged. And Hercules picked up the three golden apples, that were as big or bigger than pumpkins, and straightway set out on his journey homeward, without paying the slightest heed to the thundering tones of the giant, who bellowed after him to come back. Another forest sprang up around his feet, and grew ancient there; and again might be seen oak-trees, of six or seven centuries old, that had waxed thus aged betwixt his enormous toes.

And there stands the giant to this day; or, at any rate, there stands a mountain as tall as he, and which bears his name; and when the thunder rumbles about its summit, we may imagine it to be the voice of Giant Atlas, bellowing after Hercules!

OUSIN EUSTACE," DEMANDED Sweet Fern, who had been sitting at the story-teller's feet, with his mouth wide open, "exactly how tall was this giant?"

"O Sweet Fern, Sweet Fern!" cried the student. "Do you think that I was there, to measure him with a yard-stick? Well, if you must know to a hair's-breadth, I suppose he might be from three to fifteen miles straight upward, and that he might have seated himself on Taconic, and had Monument Mountain for a footstool."

"Dear me!" ejaculated the good little boy, with a contented sort of a grunt, "that was a giant, sure enough! And how long was his little finger?"

"As long as from Tanglewood to the lake," said Eustace.

"Sure enough, that was a giant!" repeated Sweet Fern, in an ecstasy at the precision of these measurements. "And how broad, I wonder, were the shoulders of Hercules?"

"That is what I have never been able to find out," answered the student. "But I think they must have been a great deal broader than mine, or than your father's, or than almost any shoulders which one sees nowadays."

"I wish," whispered Sweet Fern, with his mouth close to the student's ear, "that you would tell me how big were some of the oak-trees that grew between the giant's toes."

"They were bigger," said Eustace, "than the great chestnut-tree which stands beyond Captain Smith's house."

"Eustace," remarked Mr. Pringle, after some deliberation, "I find it impossible to express such an opinion of this story as will be likely to gratify, in the smallest degree, your pride of authorship. Pray let me advise you never more to meddle with a classical myth. Your imagination is altogether Gothic, and will inevitably Gothicize everything that you touch. The effect is like bedaubing a marble statue with paint. This giant, now! How can you have ventured to thrust his huge, disproportioned mass among the seemly outlines of Grecian fable, the tendency of which is to reduce even the extravagant within limits, by its pervading elegance?"

"I described the giant as he appeared to me," replied the student, rather piqued. "And, sir, if you would only bring your mind into such a relation with these fables as is necessary in order to remodel them, you would see at once that an old Greek had no more exclusive right to them than a modern Yankee has. They are the common property of the world, and of all time. The ancient poets remodeled them at pleasure, and held them plastic in their hands; and why should they not be plastic in my hands as well?"

Mr. Pringle could not forbear a smile.

"And besides," continued Eustace, "the moment you put any warmth of heart, any passion or affection, any human or divine morality, into a classic mould, you make it quite another thing from what it was before. My own opinion is, that the Greeks, by taking possession of these legends (which were the immemorial birthright of mankind), and putting them into shapes of inde-structible beauty, indeed, but cold and heartless, have done all subsequent ages an incalculable injury."

"Which you, doubtless, were born to remedy," said Mr. Pringle, laughing outright. "Well, well, go on; but take my advice, and never put any of your travesties on paper. And, as your next effort, what if you should try your hand on some one of the legends of Apollo?"

"Ah, sir, you propose it as an impossibility," observed the student, after a moment's meditation; "and, to be sure, at first thought, the idea of a Gothic Apollo strikes one rather ludicrously. But I will turn over your suggestion in my mind, and do not quite despair of success."

During the above discussion, the children (who understood not a word of it) had grown very sleepy, and were now sent off to bed. Their drowsy babble was heard, ascending the staircase, while a northwest wind roared loudly among the tree-tops of Tanglewood, and played an anthem around the house. Eustace Bright went back to the study, and again endeavored to hammer out some verses, but fell asleep between two of the rhymes.

THE MIRACVLOVS PITCHER.
THE HILL-SIDE.

INTRODVCTORY TO THE MIRACVLOVS PITCHER

ND WHEN, AND WHERE, DO YOU THINK we find the children next? No longer in the winter-time, but in the merry month of May. No longer in Tanglewood play-room, or at Tanglewood fireside, but more than halfway up a monstrous hill, or a mountain, as perhaps it would be better pleased to have us call it. They had set out from home with the mighty purpose of climbing this high hill, even to the very tiptop of its bald head. To be sure, it was not quite so high as Chimborazo or Mont Blanc, and was even a good deal lower than old Graylock. But, at any rate, it was higher than a thousand ant-hillocks or a million of mole-hills; and, when measured by the short strides of little children, might be reckoned a very respectable mountain.

And was Cousin Eustace with the party? Of that you may be certain; else how could the book go on a step farther? He was now in the middle of the spring vacation, and looked pretty much as we saw him four or five months ago, except that, if you gazed quite closely at his upper lip, you could discern the funniest little bit of a mustache upon it. Setting aside this mark of mature manhood, you might have considered Cousin Eustace just as much a boy as when you first became acquainted with him. He was as merry, as playful, as good-humored, as light of foot and of spirits, and equally a favorite with the little folks, as he had always been. This expedition up the mountain was entirely of his contrivance. All the way up the steep ascent, he had encouraged the elder children with his cheerful voice; and when Dandelion, Cowslip, and Squash-Blossom grew weary, he had lugged them along, alternately, on his back. In this manner, they had passed through the orchards and pastures on the lower part of the hill, and had reached the wood, which extends thence towards its bare summit.

The month of May, thus far, had been more amiable than it often is, and this was as sweet and genial a day as the heart of man or child could wish. In their progress up the hill, the small people had found enough of violets, blue and white, and some that were as golden as if they had the touch of Midas on them. That sociablest of flowers, the little Houstonia, was very abundant. It is a flower that never lives alone, but which loves its own kind, and is always fond of dwelling with a great many friends and relatives around it. Sometimes you see a family of them, covering a space no bigger than the palm of your hand; and sometimes a large community, whitening a whole tract of pasture, and all keeping one another in cheerful heart and life.

Within the verge of the wood there were columbines, looking more pale than red, because they were so modest, and had thought proper to seclude themselves too anxiously from the sun. There were wild geraniums, too, and a thousand white blossoms of the strawberry. The trailing arbutus was not yet quite out of bloom; but it hid its precious flowers under the last year's withered forest-leaves, as carefully as a mother-bird hides its little young ones. It knew, I suppose, how beautiful and sweet-scented they were. So cunning was their concealment, that the children sometimes smelt the delicate richness of their perfume before they knew whence it proceeded.

Amid so much new life, it was strange and truly pitiful to behold, here and there, in the fields and pastures, the hoary periwigs of dandelions that had already gone to seed. They had done with summer before the summer came. Within those small globes of winged seeds it was autumn now!

Well, but we must not waste our valuable pages with any more talk about the spring-time and wild flowers. There is something, we hope, more interesting to be talked about. If you look at the group of children, you may see them all gathered around Eustace Bright, who, sitting on the stump of a tree, seems to be just beginning a story. The fact is, the younger part of the troop have found out that it takes rather too many of their short strides to measure the long ascent of the hill. Cousin Eustace, therefore, has decided to leave Sweet Fern, Cowslip, Squash-Blossom, and Dandelion, at this point, midway up, until the return of the rest of the party from the summit. And because they complain a little, and do not quite like to stay behind, he gives them some apples out of his pocket, and proposes to tell them a very pretty story. Hereupon they brighten up, and change their grieved looks into the broadest kind of smiles.

As for the story, I was there to hear it, hidden behind a bush, and shall tell it over to you in the pages that come next.

THE·MIRACVLOVS·PITCHER

NE EVENING, IN TIMES LONG AGO, OLD Philemon and his old wife Baucis sat at their cottage-door, enjoying the calm and beautiful sunset. They had already eaten their frugal supper, and intended now to spend a quiet hour or two before bedtime. So they talked together about their garden, and their cow, and their bees, and their grapevine, which clambered over the cottage-wall, and on which the grapes were beginning to turn purple. But the rude shouts of children and the fierce barking of dogs, in the village near at hand, grew louder and louder, until, at last, it was hardly possible for Baucis and Philemon to hear each other speak.

"Ah, wife," cried Philemon, "I fear some poor traveler is seeking hospitality among our neighbors yonder, and, instead of giving him food and lodging, they have set their dogs at him, as their custom is!"

"Well-a-day!" answered old Baucis, "I do wish our neighbors felt a little more kindness for their fellow-creatures. And only

PLATE 15
Philemon and Baucis

think of bringing up their children in this naughty way, and patting them on the head when they fling stones at strangers!"

"Those children will never come to any good," said Philemon, shaking his white head. "To tell you the truth, wife, I should not wonder if some terrible thing were to happen to all the people in the village unless they mend their manners. But, as for you and me, so long as Providence affords us a crust of bread, let us be ready to give half to any poor, homeless stranger that may come along and need it."

"That's right, husband!" said Baucis. "So we will!"

These old folks, you must know, were quite poor, and had to work pretty hard for a living. Old Philemon toiled diligently in his garden, while Baucis was always busy with her distaff, or making a little butter and cheese with their cow's milk, or doing one thing and another about the cottage. Their food was seldom anything but bread, milk, and vegetables, with sometimes a portion of honey from their beehive, and now and then a bunch of grapes, that had ripened against the cottage wall. But they were two of the kindest old people in the world, and would cheerfully have gone without their dinners, any day, rather than refuse a slice of their brown loaf, a cup of new milk, and a spoonful of honey, to the weary traveler who might pause before their door. They felt as if such guests had a sort of holiness, and that they ought, therefore, to treat them better and more bountifully than their own selves.

Their cottage stood on a rising ground, at some short distance from a village, which lay in a hollow valley, that was about half a mile in breadth. This valley, in past ages, when the world was new, had probably been the bed of a lake. There, fishes had glided to and fro in the depths, and water-weeds had grown along the margin, and trees and hills had seen their reflected images in the broad and peaceful mirror. But, as the waters subsided, men had cultivated the soil, and built houses on it, so that it was now a fertile spot, and bore no traces of the ancient lake, except a very small brook, which meandered through the midst of the village, and supplied the inhabitants with water. The valley had been dry land so long, that oaks had sprung up, and grown great and high, and perished with old age, and been succeeded by others, as tall and stately as the first. Never was there a prettier or more fruitful valley. The very sight of the plenty around them should have made the inhabitants kind and gentle, and ready to show their gratitude to Providence by doing good to their fellow-creatures.

But, we are sorry to say, the people of this lovely village were not worthy to dwell in a spot on which Heaven had smiled so beneficently. They were a very selfish and hard-hearted people, and had no pity for the poor, nor sympathy with the homeless. They would only have laughed, had anybody told them that human beings owe a debt of love to one another, because there is no other method of paying the debt of love and care which all of us owe to Providence. You will hardly believe what I am going to tell you. These naughty people taught their children to be no better than themselves, and used to clap their hands, by way of encouragement, when they saw the little boys and girls run after some poor stranger, shouting at his heels and pelting him with stones. They kept large and fierce dogs, and whenever a traveler ventured to show himself in the village street, this pack of disagreeable curs scampered to meet him, barking, snarling, and showing their teeth. Then they would seize him by his leg, or by his clothes, just as it happened; and if he were ragged when he came, he was generally a pitiable object before he had time to run away. This was a very terrible thing to poor travelers, as you may suppose, especially when they chanced to be sick, or feeble, or lame, or old. Such persons (if they once knew how badly these unkind people, and their unkind children and curs, were in the habit of behaving) would go miles and miles out of their way, rather than try to pass through the village again.

What made the matter seem worse, if possible, was that when rich persons came in their chariots, or riding on beautiful horses, with their servants in rich liveries attending on them, nobody could be more civil and obsequious than the inhabitants of the village. They would take off their hats, and make the humblest bows you ever saw. If the children were rude, they were pretty certain to get their ears boxed; and as for the dogs, if a single cur in the pack presumed to yelp, his master instantly beat him with a club, and tied him up without any supper. This would have been all very well, only it proved that the villagers cared much about the money that a stranger had in his pocket, and nothing whatever for the human soul, which lives equally in the beggar and the prince.

So now you can understand why old Philemon spoke so sorrowfully, when he heard the shouts of the children and the barking of the dogs, at the farther extremity of the village street. There was a confused din, which lasted a good while, and seemed to pass quite through the breadth of the valley.

"I never heard the dogs so loud!" observed the good old man.

"Nor the children so rude!" answered his good old wife.

PLATE 16
The strangers in the village

They sat shaking their heads, one to another, while the noise came nearer and nearer; until, at the foot of the little eminence on which their cottage stood, they saw two travelers approaching on foot. Close behind them came the fierce dogs, snarling at their very heels. A little farther off, ran a crowd of children, who sent up shrill cries, and flung stones at the two strangers, with all their might. Once or twice, the younger of the two men (he was a slender and very active figure) turned about and drove back the dogs with a staff which he carried in his hand. His companion, who was a very tall person, walked calmly along, as if disdaining to notice either the naughty children, or the pack of curs, whose manners the children seemed to imitate.

Both of the travelers were very humbly clad, and looked as if they might not have money enough in their pockets to pay for a night's lodging. And this, I am afraid, was the reason why the villagers had allowed their children and dogs to treat them so rudely.

"Come, wife," said Philemon to Baucis, "let us go and meet these poor people. No doubt, they feel almost too heavy-hearted to climb the hill."

"Go you and meet them," answered Baucis, "while I make haste within doors, and see whether we can get them anything for supper. A comfortable bowl of bread and milk would do wonders towards raising their spirits."

Accordingly, she hastened into the cottage. Philemon, on his part, went forward, and extended his hand with so hospitable an aspect that there was no need of saying what nevertheless he did say, in the heartiest tone imaginable,—

"Welcome, strangers! welcome!"

"Thank you!" replied the younger of the two, in a lively kind of way, notwithstanding his weariness and trouble. "This is quite another greeting than we have met with yonder in the village. Pray, why do you live in such a bad neighborhood?"

"Ah!" observed old Philemon, with a quiet and benign smile, "Providence put me here, I hope, among other reasons, in order that I may make you what amends I can for the inhospitality of my neighbors."

"Well said, old father!" cried the traveler, laughing; "and, if the truth must be told, my companion and myself need some amends. Those children (the little rascals!) have bespattered us finely with their mud-balls; and one of the curs has torn my cloak, which was ragged enough already. But I took him across the muzzle with my staff; and I think you may have heard him yelp, even thus far off."

Philemon was glad to see him in such good spirits; nor, indeed, would you have fancied, by the traveler's look and manner, that he was weary with a long day's journey, besides being disheartened by rough treatment at the end of it. He was dressed in rather an odd way, with a sort of cap on his head, the brim of which stuck out over both ears. Though it was a summer evening, he wore a cloak, which he kept wrapt closely about him, perhaps because his under garments were shabby. Philemon perceived, too, that he had on a singular pair of shoes; but, as it was now growing dusk, and as the old man's eyesight was none the sharpest, he could not precisely tell in what the strangeness consisted. One thing, certainly, seemed queer. The traveler was so wonderfully light and active, that it appeared as if his feet sometimes rose from the ground of their own accord, or could only be kept down by an effort.

"I used to be light-footed, in my youth," said Philemon to the traveler. "But I always found my feet grow heavier towards nightfall."

"There is nothing like a good staff to help one along," answered the stranger; "and I happen to have an excellent one, as you see."

This staff, in fact, was the oddest-looking staff that Philemon had ever beheld. It was made of olive-wood, and had something like a little pair of wings near the top. Two snakes, carved in the wood, were represented as twining themselves about the staff, and were so very skillfully executed that old Philemon (whose eyes, you know, were getting rather dim) almost thought them alive, and that he could see them wriggling and twisting.

"A curious piece of work, sure enough!" said he. "A staff with wings! It would be an excellent kind of stick for a little boy to ride astride of!"

By this time, Philemon and his two guests had reached the cottage door.

"Friends," said the old man, "sit down and rest yourselves here on this bench. My good wife Baucis has gone to see what you can have for supper. We are poor folks; but you shall be welcome to whatever we have in the cupboard."

The younger stranger threw himself carelessly on the bench, letting his staff fall, as he did so. And here happened something rather marvelous, though trifling enough, too. The staff seemed to get up from the ground of its own accord, and, spreading its little pair of wings, it half hopped, half flew, and leaned itself against the wall of the cottage. There it stood quite still, except that the snakes continued to wriggle. But, in my private opinion, old Philemon's eyesight had been playing him tricks again.

Before he could ask any questions, the elder stranger drew his attention from the wonderful staff, by speaking to him.

"Was there not," asked the stranger, in a remarkably deep tone of voice, "a lake, in very ancient times, covering the spot where now stands yonder village?"

"Not in my day, friend," answered Philemon; "and yet I am an old man, as you see. There were always the fields and meadows, just as they are now, and the old trees, and the little stream murmuring through the midst of the valley. My father, nor his father before him, ever saw it otherwise, so far as I know; and doubtless it will still be the same, when old Philemon shall be gone and forgotten!"

"That is more than can be safely foretold," observed the stranger; and there was something very stern in his deep voice. He shook his head, too, so that his dark and heavy curls were shaken with the movement. "Since the inhabitants of yonder village have forgotten the affections and sympathies of their nature, it were better that the lake should be rippling over their dwellings again!"

The traveler looked so stern that Philemon was really almost frightened; the more so, that, at his frown, the twilight seemed suddenly to grow darker, and that, when he shook his head, there was a roll as of thunder in the air.

But, in a moment afterwards, the stranger's face became so kindly and mild that the old man quite forgot his terror. Nevertheless, he could not help feeling that this elder traveler must be no ordinary personage, although he happened now to be attired so humbly and to be journeying on foot. Not that Philemon fancied him a prince in disguise, or any character of that sort; but rather some exceedingly wise man, who went about the world in this poor garb, despising wealth and all worldly objects, and seeking everywhere to add a mite to his wisdom. This idea appeared the more probable, because, when Philemon raised his eyes to the stranger's face, he seemed to see more thought there, in one look, than he could have studied out in a lifetime.

While Baucis was getting the supper, the travelers both began to talk very sociably with Philemon. The younger, indeed, was extremely loquacious, and made such shrewd and witty remarks, that the good old man continually burst out a-laughing, and pronounced him the merriest fellow whom he had seen for many a day.

"Pray, my young friend," said he, as they grew familiar together, "what may I call your name?"

"Why, I am very nimble, as you see," answered the traveler. "So, if you call me Quicksilver, the name will fit tolerably well."

"Quicksilver? Quicksilver?" repeated Philemon, looking in the traveler's face, to see if he were making fun of him. "It is a very odd name! And your companion there? Has he as strange a one?"

"You must ask the thunder to tell it you!" replied Quicksilver, putting on a mysterious look. "No other voice is loud enough."

This remark, whether it were serious or in jest, might have caused Philemon to conceive a very great awe of the elder stranger, if, on venturing to gaze at him, he had not beheld so much beneficence in his visage. But, undoubtedly, here was the grandest figure that ever sat so humbly beside a cottage door. When the stranger conversed, it was with gravity, and in such a way that Philemon felt irresistibly moved to tell him everything which he had most at heart. This is always the feeling that people have, when they meet with any one wise enough to comprehend all their good and evil, and to despise not a tittle of it.

But Philemon, simple and kind-hearted old man that he was, had not many secrets to disclose. He talked, however, quite garrulously, about the events of his past life, in the whole course of which he had never been a score of miles from this very spot. His wife Baucis and himself had dwelt in the cottage from their youth upward, earning their bread by honest labor, always poor, but still contented. He told what excellent butter and cheese Baucis made, and how nice were the vegetables which he raised in his garden. He said, too, that, because they loved one another so very much, it was the wish of both that death might not separate them, but that they should die, as they had lived, together.

As the stranger listened, a smile beamed over his countenance, and made its expression as sweet as it was grand.

"You are a good old man," said he to Philemon, "and you have a good old wife to be your helpmeet. It is fit that your wish be granted."

And it seemed to Philemon, just then, as if the sunset clouds threw up a bright flash from the west, and kindled a sudden light in the sky.

Baucis had now got supper ready, and, coming to the door, began to make apologies for the poor fare which she was forced to set before her guests.

"Had we known you were coming," said she, "my good man and myself would have gone without a morsel, rather than you should lack a better supper. But I took the most part of to-day's milk to make cheese; and our last loaf is already half eaten. Ah me! I never feel the sorrow of being poor, save when a poor traveler knocks at our door."

"All will be very well; do not trouble yourself, my good dame," replied the elder stranger, kindly. "An honest, hearty welcome to a guest works miracles with the fare, and is capable of turning the coarsest food to nectar and ambrosia."

"A welcome you shall have," cried Baucis, "and likewise a little honey that we happen to have left, and a bunch of purple grapes besides."

"Why, Mother Baucis, it is a feast!" exclaimed Quicksilver, laughing, "an absolute feast! and you shall see how bravely I will play my part at it! I think I never felt hungrier in my life."

"Mercy on us!" whispered Baucis to her husband. "If the young man has such a terrible appetite, I am afraid there will not be half enough supper!"

They all went into the cottage.

And now, my little auditors, shall I tell you something that will make you open your eyes very wide? It is really one of the oddest circumstances in the whole story. Quicksilver's staff, you recollect, had set itself up against the wall of the cottage. Well; when its master entered the door, leaving this wonderful staff behind, what should it do but immediately spread its little wings, and go hopping and fluttering up the door-steps! Tap, tap, went the staff, on the kitchen floor; nor did it rest until it had stood itself on end, with the greatest gravity and decorum, beside Quicksilver's chair.

Old Philemon, however, as well as his wife, was so taken up in attending to their guests, that no notice was given to what the staff had been about.

As Baucis had said, there was but a scanty supper for two hungry travelers. In the middle of the table was the remnant of a brown loaf, with a piece of cheese on one side of it, and a dish of honeycomb on the other. There was a pretty good bunch of grapes for each of the guests. A moderately sized earthen pitcher, nearly full of milk, stood at a corner of the board; and when Baucis had filled two bowls, and set them before the strangers, only a little milk remained in the bottom of the pitcher. Alas! it is a very sad business, when a bountiful heart finds itself pinched and squeezed among narrow circumstances. Poor Baucis kept wishing that she might starve for a week to come, if it were possible, by so doing, to provide these hungry folks a more plentiful supper.

And, since the supper was so exceedingly small, she could not help wishing that their appetites had not been quite so large. Why, at their very first sitting down, the travelers both drank off all the milk in their two bowls, at a draught.

"A little more milk, kind Mother Baucis, if you please," said Quicksilver. "The day has been hot, and I am very much athirst."

"Now, my dear people," answered Baucis, in great confusion, "I am so sorry and ashamed! But the truth is, there is hardly a drop more milk in the pitcher. O husband! husband! why didn't we go without our supper?"

"Why, it appears to me," cried Quicksilver, starting up from table and taking the pitcher by the handle, "it really appears to me that matters are not quite so bad as you represent them. Here is certainly more milk in the pitcher."

So saying, and to the vast astonishment of Baucis, he proceeded to fill, not only his own bowl, but his companion's likewise, from the pitcher, that was supposed to be almost empty. The good woman could scarcely believe her eyes. She had certainly poured out nearly all the milk, and had peeped in afterwards, and seen the bottom of the pitcher, as she set it down upon the table.

"But I am old," thought Baucis to herself, "and apt to be forgetful. I suppose I must have made a mistake. At all events, the pitcher cannot help being empty now, after filling the bowls twice over."

"What excellent milk!" observed Quicksilver, after quaffing the contents of the second bowl. "Excuse me, my kind hostess, but I must really ask you for a little more."

Now Baucis had seen, as plainly as she could see anything, that Quicksilver had turned the pitcher upside down, and consequently had poured out every drop of milk, in filling the last bowl. Of course, there could not possibly be any left. However, in order to let him know precisely how the case was, she lifted the pitcher, and made a gesture as if pouring milk into Quicksilver's bowl, but without the remotest idea that any milk would stream forth. What was her surprise, therefore, when such an abundant cascade fell bubbling into the bowl, that it was immediately filled to the brim, and overflowed upon the table! The two snakes that were twisted about Quicksilver's staff (but neither Baucis nor Philemon happened to observe this circumstance) stretched out their heads, and began to lap up the spilt milk.

PLATE 17
The strangers entertained

And then what a delicious fragrance the milk had! It seemed as if Philemon's only cow must have pastured, that day, on the richest herbage that could be found anywhere in the world. I only wish that each of you, my beloved little souls, could have a bowl of such nice milk, at supper-time!

"And now a slice of your brown loaf, Mother Baucis," said Quicksilver, "and a little of that honey!"

Baucis cut him a slice, accordingly; and though the loaf, when she and her husband ate of it, had been rather too dry and crusty to be palatable, it was now as light and moist as if but a few hours out of the oven. Tasting a crumb, which had fallen on the table, she found it more delicious than bread ever was before, and could hardly believe that it was a loaf of her own kneading and baking. Yet, what other loaf could it possibly be?

But, oh the honey! I may just as well let it alone, without trying to describe how exquisitely it smelt and looked. Its color was that of the purest and most transparent gold; and it had the odor of a thousand flowers; but of such flowers as never grew in an earthly garden, and to seek which the bees must have flown high above the clouds. The wonder is, that, after alighting on a flower-bed of so delicious fragrance and immortal bloom, they should have been content to fly down again to their hive in Philemon's garden. Never was such honey tasted, seen, or smelt. The perfume floated around the kitchen, and made it so delightful, that, had you closed your eyes, you would instantly have forgotten the low ceiling and smoky walls, and have fancied yourself in an arbor, with celestial honeysuckles creeping over it.

Although good Mother Baucis was a simple old dame, she could not but think that there was something rather out of the common way, in all that had been going on. So, after helping the guests to bread and honey, and laying a bunch of grapes by each of their plates, she sat down by Philemon, and told him what she had seen, in a whisper.

"Did you ever hear the like?" asked she.

"No, I never did," answered Philemon, with a smile. "And I rather think, my dear old wife, you have been walking about in a sort of a dream. If I had poured out the milk, I should have seen through the business at once. There happened to be a little more in the pitcher than you thought,—that is all."

"Ah, husband," said Baucis, "say what you will, these are very uncommon people."

"Well, well," replied Philemon, still smiling, "perhaps they are. They certainly do look as if they had seen better days; and I am heartily glad to see them making so comfortable a supper."

Each of the guests had now taken his bunch of grapes upon his plate. Baucis (who rubbed her eyes, in order to see the more clearly) was of opinion that the clusters had grown larger and richer, and that each separate grape seemed to be on the point of bursting with ripe juice. It was entirely a mystery to her how such grapes could ever have been produced from the old stunted vine that climbed against the cottage wall.

"Very admirable grapes these!" observed Quicksilver, as he swallowed one after another, without apparently diminishing his cluster. "Pray, my good host, whence did you gather them?"

"From my own vine," answered Philemon. "You may see one of its branches twisting across the window, yonder. But wife and I never thought the grapes very fine ones."

"I never tasted better," said the guest. "Another cup of this delicious milk, if you please, and I shall then have supped better than a prince."

This time, old Philemon bestirred himself, and took up the pitcher; for he was curious to discover whether there was any reality in the marvels which Baucis had whispered to him. He knew that his good old wife was incapable of falsehood, and that she was seldom mistaken in what she supposed to be true; but this was so very singular a case, that he wanted to see into it with his own eyes. On taking up the pitcher, therefore, he slyly peeped into it, and was fully satisfied that it contained not so much as a single drop. All at once, however, he beheld a little white fountain, which gushed up from the bottom of the pitcher, and speedily filled it to the brim with foaming and deliciously fragrant milk. It was lucky that Philemon, in his surprise, did not drop the miraculous pitcher from his hand.

"Who are ye, wonder-working strangers?" cried he, even more bewildered than his wife had been.

"Your guests, my good Philemon, and your friends," replied the elder traveler, in his mild, deep voice, that had something at once sweet and awe-inspiring in it. "Give me likewise a cup of the milk; and may your pitcher never be empty for kind Baucis and yourself, any more than for the needy wayfarer!"

The supper being now over, the strangers requested to be shown to their place of repose. The old people would gladly have talked with them a little longer, and have expressed the wonder which they felt, and their delight at finding the poor and meagre supper prove so much better and more abundant than they hoped.

But the elder traveler had inspired them with such reverence, that they dared not ask him any questions. And when Philemon drew Quicksilver aside, and inquired how under the sun a fountain of milk could have got into an old earthen pitcher, this latter personage pointed to his staff.

"There is the whole mystery of the affair," quoth Quicksilver; "and if you can make it out, I'll thank you to let me know. I can't tell what to make of my staff. It is always playing such odd tricks as this; sometimes getting me a supper, and, quite as often, stealing it away. If I had any faith in such nonsense, I should say the stick was bewitched!"

He said no more, but looked so slyly in their faces, that they rather fancied he was laughing at them. The magic staff went hopping at his heels, as Quicksilver quitted the room. When left alone, the good old couple spent some little time in conversation about the events of the evening, and then lay down on the floor, and fell fast asleep. They had given up their sleeping-room to the guests, and had no other bed for themselves, save these planks, which I wish had been as soft as their own hearts.

The old man and his wife were stirring betimes in the morning, and the strangers likewise arose with the sun, and made their preparations to depart. Philemon hospitably entreated them to remain a little longer, until Baucis could milk the cow, and bake a cake upon the hearth, and, perhaps, find them a few fresh eggs, for breakfast. The guests, however, seemed to think it better to accomplish a good part of their journey before the heat of the day should come on. They, therefore, persisted in setting out immediately, but asked Philemon and Baucis to walk forth with them a short distance, and show them the road which they were to take.

So they all four issued from the cottage, chatting together like old friends. It was very remarkable, indeed, how familiar the old couple insensibly grew with the elder traveler, and how their good and simple spirits melted into his, even as two drops of water would melt into the illimitable ocean. And as for Quicksilver, with his keen, quick, laughing wits, he appeared to discover every little thought that but peeped into their minds, before they suspected it themselves. They sometimes wished, it is true, that he had not been quite so quick-witted, and also that he would fling away his staff, which looked so mysteriously mischievous, with the snakes always writhing about it. But then, again, Quicksilver showed himself so very good-humored, that they would have been rejoiced to keep him in their cottage, staff, snakes, and all, every day, and the whole day long.

"Ah me! Well-a-day!" exclaimed Philemon, when they had walked a little way from their door. "If our neighbors only knew what a blessed thing it is to show hospitality to strangers, they would tie up all their dogs, and never allow their children to fling another stone."

"It is a sin and shame for them to behave so,—that it is!" cried good old Baucis, vehemently. "And I mean to go this very day, and tell some of them what naughty people they are!"

"I fear," remarked Quicksilver, slyly smiling, "that you will find none of them at home."

The elder traveler's brow, just then, assumed such a grave, stern, and awful grandeur, yet serene withal, that neither Baucis nor Philemon dared to speak a word. They gazed reverently into his face, as if they had been gazing at the sky.

"When men do not feel towards the humblest stranger as if he were a brother," said the traveler, in tones so deep that they sounded like those of an organ, "they are unworthy to exist on earth, which was created as the abode of a great human brotherhood!"

"And, by the by, my dear old people," cried Quicksilver, with the liveliest look of fun and mischief in his eyes, "where is this same village that you talk about? On which side of us does it lie? Methinks I do not see it hereabouts."

Philemon and his wife turned towards the valley, where, at sunset, only the day before, they had seen the meadows, the houses, the gardens, the clumps of trees, the wide, green-margined street, with children playing in it, and all the tokens of business, enjoyment, and prosperity. But what was their astonishment! There was no longer any appearance of a village! Even the fertile vale, in the hollow of which it lay, had ceased to have existence. In its stead, they beheld the broad, blue surface of a lake, which filled the great basin of the valley from brim to brim, and reflected the surrounding hills in its bosom with as tranquil an image as if it had been there ever since the creation of the world. For an instant, the lake remained perfectly smooth. Then, a little breeze sprang up, and caused the water to dance, glitter, and sparkle in the early sunbeams, and to dash, with a pleasant rippling murmur, against the hither shore.

The lake seemed so strangely familiar, that the old couple were greatly perplexed, and felt as if they could only have been dreaming about a village having lain there. But, the next moment, they remembered the vanished dwellings, and the faces and characters of the inhabitants, far too distinctly for a dream. The village had been there yesterday, and now was gone!

"Alas!" cried these kind-hearted old people, "what has become of our poor neighbors?"

"They exist no longer as men and women," said the elder traveler, in his grand and deep voice, while a roll of thunder seemed to echo it at a distance. "There was neither use nor beauty in such a life as theirs; for they never softened or sweetened the hard lot of mortality by the exercise of kindly affections between man and man. They retained no image of the better life in their bosoms; therefore, the lake, that was of old, has spread itself forth again, to reflect the sky!"

"And as for those foolish people," said Quicksilver, with his mischievous smile, "they are all transformed to fishes. There needed but little change, for they were already a scaly set of rascals, and the coldest-blooded beings in existence. So, kind Mother Baucis, whenever you or your husband have an appetite for a dish of broiled trout, he can throw in a line, and pull out half a dozen of your old neighbors!"

"Ah," cried Baucis, shuddering, "I would not, for the world, put one of them on the gridiron!"

"No," added Philemon, making a wry face, "we could never relish them!"

"As for you, good Philemon," continued the elder traveler,— "and you, kind Baucis,—you, with your scanty means, have mingled so much heartfelt hospitality with your entertainment of the homeless stranger, that the milk became an inexhaustible fount of nectar, and the brown loaf and the honey were ambrosia. Thus, the divinities have feasted, at your board, off the same viands that supply their banquets on Olympus. You have done well, my dear old friends. Wherefore, request whatever favor you have most at heart, and it is granted."

Philemon and Baucis looked at one another, and then,— I know not which of the two it was who spoke, but that one uttered the desire of both their hearts.

"Let us live together, while we live, and leave the world at the same instant, when we die! For we have always loved one another!"

"Be it so!" replied the stranger, with majestic kindness. "Now, look towards your cottage!"

They did so. But what was their surprise on beholding a tall edifice of white marble, with a wide-open portal, occupying the spot where their humble residence had so lately stood!

"There is your home," said the stranger, beneficently smiling on them both. "Exercise your hospitality in yonder palace as freely as in the poor hovel to which you welcomed us last evening."

The old folks fell on their knees to thank him; but, behold! neither he nor Quicksilver was there.

So Philemon and Baucis took up their residence in the marble palace, and spent their time, with vast satisfaction to themselves, in making everybody jolly and comfortable who happened to pass that way. The milk-pitcher, I must not forget to say, retained its marvelous quality of being never empty, when it was desirable to have it full. Whenever an honest, good-humored, and free-hearted guest took a draught from this pitcher, he invariably found it the sweetest and most invigorating fluid that ever ran down his throat. But, if a cross and disagreeable curmudgeon happened to sip, he was pretty certain to twist his visage into a hard knot, and pronounce it a pitcher of sour milk!

Thus the old couple lived in their palace a great, great while, and grew older and older, and very old indeed. At length, however, there came a summer morning when Philemon and Baucis failed to make their appearance, as on other mornings, with one hospitable smile overspreading both their pleasant faces, to invite the guests of over-night to breakfast. The guests searched everywhere, from top to bottom of the spacious palace, and all to no purpose. But, after a great deal of perplexity, they espied, in front of the portal, two venerable trees, which nobody could remember to have seen there the day before. Yet there they stood, with their roots fastened deep into the soil, and a huge breadth of foliage overshadowing the whole front of the edifice. One was an oak, and the other a linden-tree. Their boughs—it was strange and beautiful to see—were intertwined together, and embraced one another, so that each tree seemed to live in the other tree's bosom much more than in its own.

While the guests were marveling how these trees, that must have required at least a century to grow, could have come to be so tall and venerable in a single night, a breeze sprang up, and set their intermingled boughs astir. And then there was a deep, broad murmur in the air, as if the two mysterious trees were speaking.

"I am old Philemon!" murmured the oak.

"I am old Baucis!" murmured the linden-tree.

But, as the breeze grew stronger, the trees both spoke at once,—"Philemon! Baucis! Baucis! Philemon!"—as if one were both and both were one, and talking together in the depths of their mutual heart. It was plain enough to perceive that the good old couple had renewed their age, and were now to spend a quiet and delightful hundred years or so, Philemon as an oak, and Baucis as a linden-tree. And oh, what a hospitable shade did they fling around them. Whenever a wayfarer paused beneath it, he heard a pleasant whisper of the leaves above his head, and wondered how the sound should so much resemble words like these:—

"Welcome, welcome, dear traveler, welcome!"

And some kind soul, that knew what would have pleased old Baucis and old Philemon best, built a circular seat around both their trunks, where, for a great while afterwards, the weary, and the hungry, and the thirsty used to repose themselves, and quaff milk abundantly out of the miraculous pitcher.

And I wish, for all our sakes, that we had the pitcher here now!

THE·HILL·SIDE·AFTER·THE·STORY·

OW MUCH DID THE PITCHER HOLD?" asked Sweet Fern.

"It did not hold quite a quart," answered the student; "but you might keep pouring milk out of it, till you should fill a hogshead, if you pleased. The truth is, it would run on forever, and not be dry even at midsummer,—which is more than can be said of yonder rill, that goes babbling down the hill-side."

"And what has become of the pitcher now?" inquired the little boy.

"It was broken, I am sorry to say, about twenty-five thousand years ago," replied Cousin Eustace. "The people mended it as well as they could, but, though it would hold milk pretty well, it was never afterwards known to fill itself of its own accord. So, you see, it was no better than any other cracked earthen pitcher."

"What a pity!" cried all the children at once.

The respectable dog Ben had accompanied the party, as did likewise a half-grown Newfoundland puppy, who went by the name of Bruin, because he was just as black as a bear. Ben, being elderly, and of very circumspect habits, was respectfully requested, by Cousin Eustace, to stay behind with the four little children, in order to keep them out of mischief. As for black Bruin, who was himself nothing but a child, the student thought it best to take him along, lest, in his rude play with the other children, he should trip them up, and send them rolling and tumbling down the hill. Advising Cowslip, Sweet Fern, Dandelion, and Squash-Blossom to sit pretty still, in the spot where he left them, the student, with Primrose and the elder children, began to ascend, and were soon out of sight among the trees.

·THE·CHIMÆRA·
·BALD·SVMMIT·

INTRODUCTORY TO
THE CHIMÆRA

PWARD, ALONG THE STEEP AND wooded hill-side, went Eustace Bright and his companions. The trees were not yet in full leaf, but had budded forth sufficiently to throw an airy shadow, while the sunshine filled them with green light. There were moss-grown rocks, half hidden among the old, brown, fallen leaves; there were rotten tree-trunks, lying at full length where they had long ago fallen; there were decayed boughs, that had been shaken down by the wintry gales, and were scattered every-where about. But still, though these things looked so aged, the aspect of the wood was that of the newest life; for, whichever way you turned your eyes, something fresh and green was springing forth, so as to be ready for the summer.

At last, the young people reached the upper verge of the wood, and found themselves almost at the summit of the hill. It was not a peak, nor a great round ball, but a pretty wide plain, or table-land, with a house and barn upon it, at some distance. That house was the home of a solitary family; and oftentimes the clouds, whence fell the rain, and whence the snow-storm drifted down into the valley, hung lower than this bleak and lonely dwelling-place.

On the highest point of the hill was a heap of stones, in the centre of which was stuck a long pole, with a little flag fluttering at the end of it. Eustace led the children thither, and bade them look around, and see how large a tract of our beautiful world they could take in at a glance. And their eyes grew wider as they looked.

Monument Mountain, to the southward, was still in the centre of the scene, but seemed to have sunk and subsided, so that it was now but an undistinguished member of a large family of hills. Beyond it, the Taconic range looked higher and bulkier than before. Our pretty lake was seen, with all its little bays and inlets; and not that alone, but two or three new lakes were opening their blue eyes to the sun. Several white villages, each with its steeple, were scattered about in the distance. There were so many farm-houses, with their acres of woodland, pasture, mowing-fields, and tillage, that the children could hardly make room in their minds to receive all these different objects. There, too, was Tanglewood, which they had hitherto thought such an important apex of the world. It now occupied so small a space, that they gazed far beyond it, and on either side, and searched a good while with all their eyes, before discovering whereabout it stood.

White, fleecy clouds were hanging in the air, and threw the dark spots of their shadow here and there over the landscape. But, by and by, the sunshine was where the shadow had been, and the shadow was somewhere else.

Far to the westward was a range of blue mountains, which Eustace Bright told the children were the Catskills. Among those misty hills, he said, was a spot where some old Dutchmen were playing an everlasting game of ninepins, and where an idle fellow, whose name was Rip Van Winkle, had fallen asleep, and slept twenty years at a stretch. The children eagerly besought Eustace to tell them all about this wonderful affair. But the student replied that the story had been told once already, and better than it ever could be told again; and that nobody would have a right to alter a word of it, until it should have grown as old as "The Gorgon's Head," and "The Three Golden Apples," and the rest of those miraculous legends.

"At least," said Periwinkle, "while we rest ourselves here, and are looking about us, you can tell us another of your own stories."

"Yes, Cousin Eustace," cried Primrose, "I advise you to tell us a story here. Take some lofty subject or other, and see if your imagination will not come up to it. Perhaps the mountain air may make you poetical, for once. And no matter how strange and wonderful the story may be, now that we are up among the clouds, we can believe anything."

"Can you believe," asked Eustace, "that there was once a winged horse?"

"Yes," said saucy Primrose; "but I am afraid you will never be able to catch him."

"For that matter, Primrose," rejoined the student, "I might possibly catch Pegasus, and get upon his back, too, as well as a dozen other fellows that I know of. At any rate, here is a story about him; and, of all places in the world, it ought certainly to be told upon a mountain-top."

So, sitting on the pile of stones, while the children clustered themselves at its base, Eustace fixed his eyes on a white cloud that was sailing by, and began as follows.

NCE, IN THE OLD, OLD TIMES (FOR all the strange things which I tell you about happened long before anybody can remember), a fountain gushed out of a hill-side, in the marvelous land of Greece. And, for aught I know, after so many thousand years, it is still gushing out of the very selfsame spot. At any rate, there was the pleasant fountain, welling freshly forth and sparkling adown the hill-side, in the golden sunset, when a handsome young man named Bellerophon drew near its margin. In his hand he held a bridle, studded with brilliant gems, and adorned with a golden bit. Seeing an old man, and another of middle age, and a little boy, near the fountain, and likewise a maiden, who was dipping up some of the water in a pitcher, he paused, and begged that he might refresh himself with a draught.

"This is very delicious water," he said to the maiden as he rinsed and filled her pitcher, after drinking out of it. "Will you be kind enough to tell me whether the fountain has any name?"

"Yes; it is called the Fountain of Pirene," answered the maiden; and then she added, "My grandmother has told me that this clear fountain was once a beautiful woman; and when her son was killed by the arrows of the huntress Diana, she melted all away into tears. And so the water, which you find so cool and sweet, is the sorrow of that poor mother's heart!"

"I should not have dreamed," observed the young stranger, "that so clear a well-spring, with its gush and gurgle, and its cheery dance out of the shade into the sunlight, had so much as one tear-drop in its bosom! And this, then, is Pirene? I thank you, pretty maiden, for telling me its name. I have come from a far-away country to find this very spot."

A middle-aged country fellow (he had driven his cow to drink out of the spring) stared hard at young Bellerophon, and at the handsome bridle which he carried in his hand.

"The water-courses must be getting low, friend, in your part of the world," remarked he, "if you come so far only to find the Fountain of Pirene. But, pray, have you lost a horse? I see you carry the bridle in your hand; and a very pretty one it is with that double row of bright stones upon it. If the horse was as fine as the bridle, you are much to be pitied for losing him."

"I have lost no horse," said Bellerophon, with a smile. "But I happen to be seeking a very famous one, which, as wise people have informed me, must be found hereabouts, if anywhere. Do you know whether the winged horse Pegasus still haunts the Fountain of Pirene, as he used to do in your forefathers' days?"

But then the country fellow laughed.

Some of you, my little friends, have probably heard that this Pegasus was a snow-white steed, with beautiful silvery wings, who spent most of his time on the summit of Mount Helicon. He was as wild, and as swift, and as buoyant, in his flight through the air, as any eagle that ever soared into the clouds. There was nothing else like him in the world. He had no mate; he never had been backed or bridled by a master; and, for many a long year, he led a solitary and a happy life.

Oh, how fine a thing it is to be a winged horse! Sleeping at night, as he did, on a lofty mountain-top, and passing the greater part of the day in the air, Pegasus seemed hardly to be a creature of the earth. Whenever he was seen, up very high above people's heads, with the sunshine on his silvery wings, you would have thought that he belonged to the sky, and that, skimming a little too low, he had got astray among our mists and vapors, and was seeking his way back again. It was very pretty to behold him plunge into the fleecy bosom of a bright cloud, and be lost in it, for a moment or two, and then break forth from the other side. Or, in a sullen rain-storm, when there was a gray pavement of clouds over the whole sky, it would sometimes happen that the winged horse descended right through it, and the glad light of the upper region would gleam after him. In another instant, it is true, both Pegasus and the pleasant light would be gone away together. But any one that was fortunate enough to see this wondrous spectacle felt cheerful the whole day afterwards, and as much longer as the storm lasted.

In the summer-time, and in the beautifullest of weather, Pegasus often alighted on the solid earth, and, closing his silvery wings, would gallop over hill and dale for pastime, as fleetly as the wind. Oftener than in any other place, he had been seen near the Fountain of Pirene, drinking the delicious water, or rolling himself upon the soft grass of the margin. Sometimes, too (but Pegasus was very dainty in his food), he would crop a few of the clover-blossoms that happened to be sweetest.

To the Fountain of Pirene, therefore, people's great-grandfathers had been in the habit of going (as long as they were youthful, and retained their faith in winged horses), in hopes of getting a glimpse at the beautiful Pegasus. But, of late years, he had been very seldom seen. Indeed, there were many of the country folks, dwelling within half an hour's walk of the fountain, who had never beheld Pegasus, and did not believe that there was any such creature in existence. The country fellow to whom Bellerophon was speaking chanced to be one of those incredulous persons.

And that was the reason why he laughed.

"Pegasus, indeed!" cried he, turning up his nose as high as such a flat nose could be turned up,—"Pegasus, indeed! A winged horse, truly! Why, friend, are you in your senses? Of what use would wings be to a horse? Could he drag the plow so well, think you? To be sure, there might be a little saving in the expense of shoes; but then, how would a man like to see his horse flying out of the stable window?—yes, or whisking up him above the clouds, when he only wanted to ride to mill? No, no! I don't believe in Pegasus. There never was such a ridiculous kind of a horse-fowl made!"

"I have some reason to think otherwise," said Bellerophon, quietly.

And then he turned to an old, gray man, who was leaning on a staff, and listening very attentively, with his head stretched forward, and one hand at his ear, because, for the last twenty years, he had been getting rather deaf.

PLATE 18
Bellerophon at the fountain

"And what say you, venerable sir?" inquired he. "In your younger days, I should imagine, you must frequently have seen the winged steed!"

"Ah, young stranger, my memory is very poor!" said the aged man. "When I was a lad, if I remember rightly, I used to believe there was such a horse, and so did everybody else. But, nowadays, I hardly know what to think, and very seldom think about the winged horse at all. If I ever saw the creature, it was a long, long while ago; and, to tell you the truth, I doubt whether I ever did see him. One day, to be sure, when I was quite a youth, I remember seeing some hoof-tramps round about the brink of the fountain. Pegasus might have made those hoof-marks; and so might some other horse."

"And have you never seen him, my fair maiden?" asked Bellerophon of the girl, who stood with the pitcher on her head, while this talk went on. "You certainly could see Pegasus, if anybody can, for your eyes are very bright."

"Once I thought I saw him," replied the maiden, with a smile and a blush. "It was either Pegasus, or a large white bird, a very great way up in the air. And one other time, as I was coming to the fountain with my pitcher, I heard a neigh. Oh, such a brisk and melodious neigh as that was! My very heart leaped with delight at the sound. But it startled me, nevertheless; so that I ran home without filling my pitcher."

"That was truly a pity!" said Bellerophon.

And he turned to the child, whom I mentioned at the beginning of the story, and who was gazing at him, as children are apt to gaze at strangers, with his rosy mouth wide open.

"Well, my little fellow," cried Bellerophon, playfully pulling one of his curls, "I suppose you have often seen the winged horse."

"That I have," answered the child, very readily. "I saw him yesterday, and many times before."

"You are a fine little man!" said Bellerophon, drawing the child closer to him. "Come, tell me all about it."

"Why," replied the child, "I often come here to sail little boats in the fountain, and to gather pretty pebbles out of its basin. And sometimes, when I look down into the water, I see the image of the winged horse, in the picture of the sky that is there. I wish he would come down, and take me on his back, and let me ride him up to the moon! But, if I so much as stir to look at him, he flies far away out of sight."

And Bellerophon put his faith in the child, who had seen the image of Pegasus in the water, and in the maiden, who had heard him neigh so melodiously, rather than in the middle-aged clown, who believed only in cart-horses, or in the old man who had forgotten the beautiful things of his youth.

Therefore, he haunted about the Fountain of Pirene for a great many days afterwards. He kept continually on the watch, looking upward at the sky, or else down into the water, hoping forever that he should see either the reflected image of the winged horse, or the marvelous reality. He held the bridle, with its bright gems and golden bit, always ready in his hand. The rustic people, who dwelt in the neighborhood, and drove their cattle to the fountain to drink, would often laugh at poor Bellerophon, and sometimes take him pretty severely to task. They told him that an able-bodied young man, like himself, ought to have better business than to be wasting his time in such an idle pursuit. They offered to sell him a horse, if he wanted one; and when Bellerophon declined the purchase, they tried to drive a bargain with him for his fine bridle.

Even the country boys thought him so very foolish, that they used to have a great deal of sport about him, and were rude enough not to care a fig, although Bellerophon saw and heard it. One little urchin, for example, would play Pegasus, and cut the oddest imaginable capers, by way of flying; while one of his schoolfellows would scamper after him, holding forth a twist of bulrushes, which was intended to represent Bellerophon's ornamental bridle. But the gentle child, who had seen the picture of Pegasus in the water, comforted the young stranger more than all the naughty boys could torment him. The dear little fellow, in his play-hours, often sat down beside him, and, without speaking a word, would look down into the fountain and up towards the sky, with so innocent a faith, that Bellerophon could not help feeling encouraged.

Now you will, perhaps, wish to be told why it was that Bellerophon had undertaken to catch the winged horse. And we shall find no better opportunity to speak about this matter than while he is waiting for Pegasus to appear.

If I were to relate the whole of Bellerophon's previous adventures, they might easily grow into a very long story. It will be quite enough to say, that, in a certain country of Asia, a terrible monster, called a Chimæra, had made its appearance, and was doing more mischief than could be talked about between now and sunset. According to the best accounts which I have been able to obtain, this Chimæra was nearly, if not quite, the ugliest and most poisonous creature, and the strangest and unaccountablest, and the hardest to fight with, and the most difficult to run away from, that ever came out of the earth's inside. It had a tail like a boa-constrictor; its body was like I do not care what; and it had three separate heads, one of which was a lion's, the second a goat's, and the third an abominably great snake's. And a hot blast of fire came flaming out of each of its three mouths! Being an earthly monster, I doubt whether it had any wings; but, wings or no, it ran like a goat and a lion, and wriggled along like a serpent, and thus contrived to make about as much speed as all the three together.

Oh, the mischief, and mischief, and mischief that this naughty creature did! With its flaming breath, it could set a forest on fire, or burn up a field of grain, or, for that matter, a village, with all its fences and houses. It laid waste the whole country round about, and used to eat up people and animals alive, and cook them afterwards in the burning oven of its stomach. Mercy on us, little children, I hope neither you nor I will ever happen to meet a Chimæra!

While the hateful beast (if a beast we can anywise call it) was doing all these horrible things, it so chanced that Bellerophon came to that part of the world, on a visit to the king. The king's name was Iobates, and Lycia was the country which he ruled over. Bellerophon was one of the bravest youths in the world, and desired nothing so much as to do some valiant and beneficent deed, such as would make all mankind admire and love him. In those days, the only way for a young man to distinguish himself was by fighting battles, either with the enemies of his country, or with wicked giants, or with troublesome dragons, or with wild beasts, when he could find nothing more dangerous to encounter. King Iobates, perceiving the courage of his youthful visitor, proposed to him to go and fight the Chimæra, which everybody else was afraid of, and which, unless it should be soon killed, was likely to convert Lycia into a desert. Bellerophon hesitated not a moment, but assured the king that he would either slay this dreaded Chimæra, or perish in the attempt.

But, in the first place, as the monster was so prodigiously swift, he bethought himself that he should never win the victory by fighting on foot. The wisest thing he could do, therefore, was to get the very best and fleetest horse that could anywhere be found. And what other horse, in all the world, was half so fleet as the marvelous horse Pegasus, who had wings as well as legs, and was even more active in the air than on the earth? To be sure, a great many people denied that there was any such horse with wings, and said that the stories about him were all poetry and nonsense. But, wonderful as it appeared, Bellerophon believed that Pegasus was a real steed, and hoped that he himself might be fortunate enough to find him; and, once fairly mounted on his back, he would be able to fight the Chimæra at better advantage.

And this was the purpose with which he had traveled from Lycia to Greece, and had brought the beautifully ornamented bridle in his hand. It was an enchanted bridle. If he could only succeed in putting the golden bit into the mouth of Pegasus, the winged horse would be submissive, and would own Bellerophon for his master, and fly whithersoever he might choose to turn therein.

But, indeed, it was a weary and anxious time, while Bellerophon waited and waited for Pegasus, in hopes that he would come and drink at the Fountain of Pirene. He was afraid lest King Iobates should imagine that he had fled from the Chimæra. It pained him, too, to think how much mischief the monster was doing, while he himself, instead of fighting with it, was compelled to sit idly poring over the bright waters of Pirene, as they gushed out of the sparkling sand. And as Pegasus came thither so seldom in these latter years, and scarcely alighted there more than once in a lifetime, Bellerophon feared that he might grow an old man, and have no strength left in his arms nor courage in his heart, before the winged horse would appear. Oh, how heavily passes the time, while an adventurous youth is yearning to do his part in life, and to gather in the harvest of his renown! How hard a lesson it is to wait! Our life is brief, and how much of it is spent in teaching us only this!

Well was it for Bellerophon that the gentle child had grown so fond of him, and was never weary of keeping him company. Every morning the child gave him a new hope to put in his bosom, instead of yesterday's withered one.

"Dear Bellerophon," he would cry, looking up hopefully into his face, "I think we shall see Pegasus to-day!"

And, at length, if it had not been for the little boy's unwavering faith, Bellerophon would have given up all hope, and would have gone back to Lycia, and have done his best to slay the Chimæra without the help of the winged horse. And in that case poor Bellerophon would at least have been terribly scorched by the creature's breath, and would most probably have been killed and devoured. Nobody should ever try to fight an earth-born Chimæra, unless he can first get upon the back of an aerial steed.

One morning the child spoke to Bellerophon even more hopefully than usual.

"Dear, dear Bellerophon," cried he, "I know not why it is, but I feel as if we should certainly see Pegasus to-day!"

And all that day he would not stir a step from Bellerophon's side; so they ate a crust of bread together, and drank some of the water of the fountain. In the afternoon, there they sat, and Bellerophon had thrown his arm around the child, who likewise had put one of his little hands into Bellerophon's. The latter was lost in his own thoughts, and was fixing his eyes vacantly on the trunks of the trees that overshadowed the fountain, and on the grapevines that clambered up among their branches. But the gentle child was gazing down into the water; he was grieved, for Bellerophon's sake, that the hope of another day should be deceived, like so many before it; and two or three quiet tear-drops fell from his eyes, and mingled with what were said to be the many tears of Pirene, when she wept for her slain children.

But, when he least thought of it, Bellerophon felt the pressure of the child's little hand, and heard a soft, almost breathless, whisper.

"See there, dear Bellerophon! There is an image in the water!"

The young man looked down into the dimpling mirror of the fountain, and saw what he took to be the reflection of a bird which seemed to be flying at a great height in the air, with a gleam of sunshine on its snowy or silvery wings.

"What a splendid bird it must be!" said he. "And how very large it looks, though it must really be flying higher than the clouds!"

"It makes me tremble!" whispered the child. "I am afraid to look up into the air! It is very beautiful, and yet I dare only look at its image in the water. Dear Bellerophon, do you not see that it is no bird? It is the winged horse Pegasus!"

Bellerophon's heart began to throb! He gazed keenly upward, but could not see the winged creature, whether bird or horse; because, just then, it had plunged into the fleecy depths of a summer cloud. It was but a moment, however, before the object reappeared, sinking lightly down out of the cloud, although still at a vast distance from the earth. Bellerophon caught the child in his arms, and shrank back with him, so that they were both hidden among the thick shrubbery which grew all around the fountain. Not that he was afraid of any harm, but he dreaded lest, if Pegasus caught a glimpse of them, he would fly far away, and alight in some inaccessible mountain-top. For it was really the winged horse. After they had expected him so long, he was coming to quench his thirst with the water of Pirene.

Nearer and nearer came the aerial wonder, flying in great circles, as you may have seen a dove when about to alight. Downward came Pegasus, in those wide, sweeping circles, which grew narrower, and narrower still, as he gradually approached the earth. The nigher the view of him, the more beautiful he was, and the more marvelous the sweep of his silvery wings. At last, with so light a pressure as hardly to bend the grass about the fountain, or imprint a hoof-tramp in the sand of its margin, he alighted, and, stooping his wild head, began to drink. He drew in the water, with long and pleasant sighs, and tranquil pauses of enjoyment; and then another draught, and another, and another. For, nowhere in the world, or up among the clouds, did Pegasus love any water as he loved this of Pirene. And when his thirst was slaked, he cropped a few of the honey-blossoms of the clover, delicately tasting them, but not caring to make a hearty meal, because the herbage, just beneath the clouds, on the lofty sides of Mount Helicon, suited his palate better than this ordinary grass.

After thus drinking to his heart's content, and, in his dainty fashion, condescending to take a little food, the winged horse began to caper to and fro, and dance as it were, out of mere idleness and sport. There never was a more playful creature made than this very Pegasus. So there he frisked, in a way that it delights me to think about, fluttering his great wings as lightly as ever did a linnet, and running little races, half on earth and half in air, and which I know not whether to call a flight or a gallop. When a creature is perfectly able to fly, he sometimes chooses to run, just for the pastime of the thing; and so did Pegasus, although it cost him some little trouble to keep his hoofs so near the ground. Bellerophon, meanwhile, holding the child's hand, peeped forth from the shrubbery, and thought that never was any sight so beautiful as this, nor ever a horse's eyes so wild and spirited as those of Pegasus. It seemed a sin to think of bridling him and riding on his back.

Once or twice, Pegasus stopped, and snuffed the air, pricking up his ears, tossing his head, and turning it on all sides, as if he partly suspected some mischief or other. Seeing nothing, however, and hearing no sound, he soon began his antics again.

At length—not that he was weary, but only idle and luxurious—Pegasus folded his wings, and lay down on the soft green turf. But, being too full of aerial life to remain quiet for many moments together, he soon rolled over on his back, with his four slender legs in the air. It was beautiful to see him, this one solitary creature, whose mate had never been created, but who needed no companion, and, living a great many hundred years, was as happy as the centuries were long. The more he did such things as mortal horses are accustomed to do, the less earthly and the more wonderful he seemed. Bellerophon and the child almost held their breath, partly from a delightful awe, but still more because they dreaded lest the slightest stir or murmur should send him up, with the speed of an arrow-flight, into the farthest blue of the sky.

Finally, when he had had enough of rolling over and over, Pegasus turned himself about, and, indolently, like any other horse, put out his fore legs, in order to rise from the ground; and Bellerophon, who had guessed that he would do so, darted suddenly from the thicket, and leaped astride of his back.

Yes, there he sat, on the back of the winged horse!

But what a bound did Pegasus make, when, for the first time, he felt the weight of a mortal man upon his loins! A bound, indeed! Before he had time to draw a breath, Bellerophon found himself five hundred feet aloft, and still shooting upward, while the winged horse snorted and trembled with terror and anger. Upward he went, up, up, up, until he plunged into the cold misty bosom of a cloud, at which, only a little while before, Bellerophon had been gazing, and fancying it a very pleasant spot. Then again, out of the heart of the cloud, Pegasus shot down like a thunderbolt, as if he meant to dash both himself and his rider headlong against a rock. Then he went through about a thousand of the wildest caprioles that had ever been performed either by a bird or a horse.

I cannot tell you half that he did. He skimmed straight forward, and sideways, and backward. He reared himself erect, with his fore legs on a wreath of mist, and his hind legs on nothing at all. He flung out his heels behind, and put down his head between his legs, with his wings pointing right upward. At about two miles' height above the earth, he turned a somerset, so that Bellerophon's heels were where his head should have been, and he seemed to look down into the sky, instead of up. He twisted his head about, and, looking Bellerophon in the face, with fire flashing from his eyes, made a terrible attempt to bite him. He fluttered his pinions so wildly that one of the silver feathers was shaken out, and, floating earthward, was picked up by the child, who kept it as long as he lived, in memory of Pegasus and Bellerophon.

But the latter (who, as you may judge, was as good a horseman as ever galloped) had been watching his opportunity, and at last clapped the golden bit of the enchanted bridle between the winged steed's jaws. No sooner was this done, than Pegasus became as manageable as if he had taken food, all his life, out of Bellerophon's hand. To speak what I really feel, it was almost a sadness to see so wild a creature grow suddenly so tame. And Pegasus seemed to feel it so, likewise. He looked round to Bellerophon, with the tears in his beautiful eyes, instead of the fire that so recently flashed from them. But when Bellerophon patted his head, and spoke a few authoritative, yet kind and soothing words, another look came into the eyes of Pegasus; for he was glad at heart, after so many lonely centuries, to have found a companion and a master.

Thus it always is with winged horses, and with all such wild and solitary creatures. If you can catch and overcome them, it is the surest way to win their love.

While Pegasus had been doing his utmost to shake Bellerophon off his back, he had flown a very long distance; and they had come within sight of a lofty mountain by the time the bit was in his mouth. Bellerophon had seen this mountain before, and knew it to be Helicon, on the summit of which was the winged horse's abode. Thither (after looking gently into his rider's face, as if to ask leave) Pegasus now flew, and, alighting, waited patiently until

Bellerophon should please to dismount. The young man, accordingly, leaped from his steed's back, but still held him fast by the bridle. Meeting his eyes, however, he was so affected by the gentleness of his aspect, and by the thought of the free life which Pegasus had heretofore lived, that he could not bear to keep him a prisoner, if he really desired his liberty.

Obeying this generous impulse he slipped the enchanted bridle off the head of Pegasus, and took the bit from his mouth.

"Leave me, Pegasus!" said he. "Either leave me, or love me."

In an instant, the winged horse shot almost out of sight, soaring straight upward from the summit of Mount Helicon. Being long after sunset, it was now twilight on the mountain-top, and dusky evening over all the country round about. But Pegasus flew so high that he overtook the departed day, and was bathed in the upper radiance of the sun. Ascending higher and higher, he looked like a bright speck, and, at last, could no longer be seen in the hollow waste of the sky. And Bellerophon was afraid that he should never behold him more. But, while he was lamenting his own folly, the bright speck reappeared, and drew nearer and nearer, until it descended lower than the sunshine; and, behold, Pegasus had come back! After this trial there was no more fear of the winged horse's making his escape. He and Bellerophon were friends, and put loving faith in one another.

That night they lay down and slept together, with Bellerophon's arm about the neck of Pegasus, not as a caution, but for kindness. And they awoke at peep of day, and bade one another good morning, each in his own language.

In this manner, Bellerophon and the wondrous steed spent several days, and grew better acquainted and fonder of each other all the time. They went on long aerial journeys, and sometimes ascended so high that the earth looked hardly bigger than—the moon. They visited distant countries, and amazed the inhabitants, who thought that the beautiful young man, on the back of the winged horse, must have come down out of the sky. A thousand miles a day was no more than an easy space for the fleet Pegasus to pass over. Bellerophon was delighted with this kind of life, and would have liked nothing better than to live always in the same way, aloft in the clear atmosphere; for it was always sunny weather up there, however cheerless and rainy it might be in the lower region. But he could not forget the horrible Chimæra, which he had promised King Iobates to slay. So, at last, when he had become well accustomed to feats of horsemanship in the air, and could manage Pegasus with the least motion of his hand, and had taught him to obey his voice, he determined to attempt the performance of this perilous adventure.

At daybreak, therefore, as soon as he unclosed his eyes, he gently pinched the winged horse's ear, in order to arouse him. Pegasus immediately started from the ground, and pranced about a quarter of a mile aloft, and made a grand sweep around the mountain-top, by way of showing that he was wide awake, and ready for any kind of an excursion. During the whole of this little flight, he uttered a loud, brisk, and melodious neigh, and finally came down at Bellerophon's side, as lightly as ever you saw a sparrow hop upon a twig.

"Well done, dear Pegasus! well done, my sky-skimmer!" cried Bellerophon, fondly stroking the horse's neck. "And now, my fleet and beautiful friend, we must break our fast. To-day we are to fight the terrible Chimæra."

As soon as they had eaten their morning meal, and drank some sparkling water from a spring called Hippocrene, Pegasus held out his head, of his own accord, so that his master might put on the bridle. Then, with a great many playful leaps and airy caperings, he showed his impatience to be gone; while Bellerophon was girding on his sword, and hanging his shield about his neck, and preparing himself for battle. When everything was ready, the rider mounted, and (as was his custom, when going a long distance) ascended five miles perpendicularly, so as the better to see whither he was directing his course. He then turned the head of Pegasus towards the east, and set out for Lycia. In their flight they overtook an eagle, and came so nigh him, before he could get out of their way, that Bellerophon might easily have caught him by the leg. Hastening onward at this rate, it was still early in the forenoon when they beheld the lofty mountains of Lycia, with their deep and shaggy valleys. If Bellerophon had been told truly, it was in one of those dismal valleys that the hideous Chimæra had taken up its abode.

Being now so near their journey's end, the winged horse gradually descended with his rider; and they took advantage of some clouds that were floating over the mountain-tops, in order to conceal themselves. Hovering on the upper surface of a cloud, and peeping over its edge, Bellerophon had a pretty distinct view of the mountainous part of Lycia, and could look into all its shadowy vales at once. At first there appeared to be nothing remarkable. It was a wild, savage, and rocky tract of high and precipitous hills. In the more level part of the country, there were the ruins of houses that had been burnt, and, here and there, the carcasses of dead cattle, strewn about the pastures where they had been feeding.

"The Chimæra must have done this mischief," thought Bellerophon. "But where can the monster be?"

As I have already said, there was nothing remarkable to be detected, at first sight, in any of the valleys and dells that lay among the precipitous heights of the mountains. Nothing at all; unless, indeed, it were three spires of black smoke, which issued from what seemed to be the mouth of a cavern, and clambered sullenly into the atmosphere. Before reaching the mountain-top, these three black smoke-wreaths mingled themselves into one. The cavern was almost directly beneath the winged horse and his rider, at the distance of about a thousand feet. The smoke, as it crept heavily upward, had an ugly, sulphurous, stifling scent, which caused Pegasus to snort and Bellerophon to sneeze. So disagreeable was it to the marvelous steed (who was accustomed to breathe only the purest air), that he waved his wings, and shot half a mile out of the range of this offensive vapor.

But, on looking behind him, Bellerophon saw something that induced him first to draw the bridle, and then to turn Pegasus about. He made a sign, which the winged horse understood, and sunk slowly through the air, until his hoofs were scarcely more than a man's height above the rocky bottom of the valley. In front, as far off as you could throw a stone, was the cavern's mouth, with the three smoke-wreaths oozing out of it. And what else did Bellerophon behold there?

There seemed to be a heap of strange and terrible creatures curled up within the cavern. Their bodies lay so close together, that Bellerophon could not distinguish them apart; but, judging by their heads, one of these creatures was a huge snake, the second a fierce lion, and the third an ugly goat. The lion and the goat were asleep; the snake was broad awake, and kept staring around him with a great pair of fiery eyes. But—and this was the most wonderful part of the matter—the three spires of smoke evidently issued from the nostrils of these three heads! So strange was the spectacle, that, though Bellerophon had been all along expecting it, the truth did not immediately occur to him, that here was the terrible three-headed Chimæra. He had found out the Chimæra's cavern. The snake, the lion, and the goat, as he supposed them to be, were not three separate creatures, but one monster!

The wicked, hateful thing! Slumbering as two thirds of it were, it still held, in its abominable claws, the remnant of an unfortunate lamb,—or possibly (but I hate to think so) it was a dear little boy,—which its three mouths had been gnawing, before two of them fell asleep!

All at once, Bellerophon started as from a dream, and knew it to be the Chimæra. Pegasus seemed to know it, at the same instant, and sent forth a neigh, that sounded like the call of a trumpet to battle. At this sound the three heads reared themselves erect, and belched out great flashes of flame. Before Bellerophon had time to consider what to do next, the monster flung itself out of the cavern and sprung straight towards him, with its immense claws extended, and its snaky tail twisting itself venomously behind. If Pegasus had not been as nimble as a bird, both he and his rider would have been overthrown by the Chimæra's headlong rush, and thus the battle have been ended before it was well begun. But the winged horse was not to be caught so. In the twinkling of an eye he was up aloft, halfway to the clouds, snorting with anger. He shuddered, too, not with affright, but with utter disgust at the loathsomeness of this poisonous thing with three heads.

NATHANIEL HAWTHORNE 191

The Chimæra, on the other hand, raised itself up so as to stand absolutely on the tip-end of its tail, with its talons pawing fiercely in the air, and its three heads spluttering fire at Pegasus and his rider. My stars, how it roared, and hissed, and bellowed! Bellerophon, meanwhile, was fitting his shield on his arm, and drawing his sword.

"Now, my beloved Pegasus," he whispered in the winged horse's ear, "thou must help me to slay this insufferable monster; or else thou shalt fly back to thy solitary mountain-peak without thy friend Bellerophon. For either the Chimæra dies, or its three mouths shall gnaw this head of mine, which has slumbered upon thy neck!"

Pegasus whinnied, and, turning back his head, rubbed his nose tenderly against his rider's cheek. It was his way of telling him that, though he had wings and was an immortal horse, yet he would perish, if it were possible for immortality to perish, rather than leave Bellerophon behind.

"I thank you, Pegasus," answered Bellerophon. "Now, then, let us make a dash at the monster!"

Uttering these words, he shook the bridle; and Pegasus darted down aslant, as swift as the flight of an arrow, right towards the Chimæra's three-fold head, which, all this time, was poking itself as high as it could into the air. As he came within arm's-length, Bellerophon made a cut at the monster, but was carried onward by his steed, before he could see whether the blow had been successful. Pegasus continued his course, but soon wheeled round, at about the same distance from the Chimæra as before. Bellerophon then perceived that he had cut the goat's head of the monster almost off, so that it dangled downward by the skin, and seemed quite dead.

But, to make amends, the snake's head and the lion's head had taken all the fierceness of the dead one into themselves, and spit flame, and hissed, and roared, with a vast deal more fury than before.

"Never mind, my brave Pegasus!" cried Bellerophon. "With another stroke like that, we will stop either its hissing or its roaring."

And again he shook the bridle. Dashing aslantwise, as before, the winged horse made another arrow-flight towards the Chimæra, and Bellerophon aimed another downright stroke at one of the two remaining heads, as he shot by. But this time, neither he nor Pegasus escaped so well as at first. With one of its claws, the Chimæra had given the young man a deep scratch in his shoulder, and had slightly damaged the left wing of the flying steed with the other. On his part, Bellerophon had mortally wounded the lion's head of the monster, insomuch that it now hung downward, with its fire almost extinguished, and sending out gasps of thick black smoke. The snake's head, however (which was the only one now left), was twice as fierce and venomous as ever before. It belched forth shoots of fire five hundred yards long, and emitted hisses so loud, so harsh, and so ear-piercing, that King Iobates heard them, fifty miles off, and trembled till the throne shook under him.

"Well-a-day!" thought the poor king; "the Chimæra is certainly coming to devour me!"

Meanwhile Pegasus had again paused in the air, and neighed angrily, while sparkles of a pure crystal flame darted out of his eyes. How unlike the lurid fire of the Chimæra! The aerial steed's spirit was all aroused, and so was that of Bellerophon.

"Dost thou bleed, my immortal horse?" cried the young man, caring less for his own hurt than for the anguish of this glorious

PLATE 19
Bellerophon slays the Chimæra

creature, that ought never to have tasted pain. "The execrable Chimæra shall pay for this mischief with his last head!"

Then he shook the bridle, shouted loudly, and guided Pegasus, not aslantwise as before, but straight at the monster's hideous front. So rapid was the onset, that it seemed but a dazzle and a flash before Bellerophon was at close gripes with his enemy.

The Chimæra, by this time, after losing its second head, had got into a red-hot passion of pain and rampant rage. It so flounced about, half on earth and partly in the air, that it was impossible to say which element it rested upon. It opened its snake-jaws to such an abominable width, that Pegasus might almost, I was going to say, have flown right down its throat, wings outspread, rider and all! At their approach it shot out a tremendous blast of its fiery breath, and enveloped Bellerophon and his steed in a perfect atmosphere of flame, singeing the wings of Pegasus, scorching off one whole side of the young man's golden ringlets, and making them both far hotter than was comfortable, from head to foot.

But this was nothing to what followed.

When the airy rush of the winged horse had brought him within the distance of a hundred yards, the Chimæra gave a spring, and flung its huge, awkward, venomous, and utterly detestable carcass right upon poor Pegasus, clung round him with might and main, and tied up its snaky tail into a knot! Up flew the aerial steed, higher, higher, higher, above the mountain-peaks, above the clouds, and almost out of sight of the solid earth. But still the earth-born monster kept its hold, and was borne upward, along with the creature of light and air. Bellerophon, meanwhile, turning about, found himself face to face with the ugly grimness of the Chimæra's visage, and could only avoid being scorched to death, or bitten right in twain, by holding up his shield. Over the upper edge of the shield, he looked sternly into the savage eyes of the monster.

But the Chimæra was so mad and wild with pain, that it did not guard itself so well as might else have been the case. Perhaps, after all, the best way to fight a Chimæra is by getting as close to it as you can. In its efforts to stick its horrible iron claws into its enemy, the creature left its own breast quite exposed; and perceiving this, Bellerophon thrust his sword up to the hilt into its cruel heart. Immediately the snaky tail untied its knot. The monster let go its hold of Pegasus, and fell from that vast height, downward; while the fire within its bosom, instead of being put out, burned fiercer than ever, and quickly began to consume the dead carcass. Thus it fell out of the sky, all a-flame, and (it being nightfall before it reached the earth) was mistaken for a shooting star or a comet. But, at early sunrise, some cottagers were going to their day's labor, and saw, to their astonishment, that several acres of ground were strewn with black ashes. In the middle of a field, there was a heap of whitened bones, a great deal higher than a haystack. Nothing else was ever seen of the dreadful Chimæra!

And when Bellerophon had won the victory, he bent forward and kissed Pegasus, while the tears stood in his eyes.

"Back now, my beloved steed!" said he. "Back to the Fountain of Pirene!"

Pegasus skimmed through the air, quicker than ever he did before, and reached the fountain in a very short time. And there he found the old man leaning on his staff, and the country fellow watering his cow, and the pretty maiden filling her pitcher.

"I remember now," quoth the old man, "I saw this winged horse once before, when I was quite a lad. But he was ten times handsomer in those days."

"I own a cart-horse, worth three of him!" said the country fellow. "If this pony were mine, the first thing I should do would be to clip his wings!"

But the poor maiden said nothing, for she had always the luck to be afraid at the wrong time. So she ran away, and let her pitcher tumble down, and broke it.

"Where is the gentle child," asked Bellerophon, "who used to keep me company, and never lost his faith, and never was weary of gazing into the fountain?"

"Here am I, dear Bellerophon!" said the child, softly.

For the little boy had spent day after day, on the margin of Pirene, waiting for his friend to come back; but when he perceived Bellerophon descending through the clouds, mounted on the winged horse, he had shrunk back into the shrubbery. He was a delicate and tender child, and dreaded lest the old man and the country fellow should see the tears gushing from his eyes.

"Thou hast won the victory," said he, joyfully, running to the knee of Bellerophon, who still sat on the back of Pegasus. "I knew thou wouldst."

"Yes, dear child!" replied Bellerophon, alighting from the winged horse. "But if thy faith had not helped me, I should never have waited for Pegasus, and never have gone up above the clouds, and never have conquered the terrible Chimæra. Thou, my beloved little friend, hast done it all. And now let us give Pegasus his liberty."

So he slipped off the enchanted bridle from the head of the marvelous steed.

"Be free, forevermore, my Pegasus!" cried he, with a shade of sadness in his tone. "Be as free as thou art fleet!"

But Pegasus rested his head on Bellerophon's shoulder, and would not be persuaded to take flight.

"Well then," said Bellerophon, caressing the airy horse, "thou shalt be with me, as long as thou wilt; and we will go together, forthwith, and tell King Iobates that the Chimæra is destroyed."

Then Bellerophon embraced the gentle child, and promised to come to him again, and departed. But, in after years, that child took higher flights upon the aerial steed than ever did Bellerophon, and achieved more honorable deeds than his friend's victory over the Chimæra. For, gentle and tender as he was, he grew to be a mighty poet!

USTACE BRIGHT TOLD THE LEGEND OF Bellerophon with as much fervor and animation as if he had really been taking a gallop on the winged horse. At the conclusion, he was gratified to discern, by the glowing countenances of his auditors, how greatly they had been interested. All their eyes were dancing in their heads, except those of Primrose. In her eyes there were positively tears; for she was conscious of something in the legend which the rest of them were not yet old enough to feel. Child's story as it was, the student had contrived to breathe through it the ardor, the generous hope, and the imaginative enterprise of youth.

"I forgive you, now, Primrose," said he, "for all your ridicule of myself and my stories. One tear pays for a great deal of laughter."

"Well, Mr. Bright," answered Primrose, wiping her eyes, and giving him another of her mischievous smiles, "it certainly does elevate your ideas, to get your head above the clouds. I advise you never to tell another story, unless it be, as at present, from the top of a mountain."

"Or from the back of Pegasus," replied Eustace, laughing. "Don't you think that I succeeded pretty well in catching that wonderful pony?"

"It was so like one of your madcap pranks!" cried Primrose, clapping her hands. "I think I see you now on his back, two miles high, and with your head downward! It is well that you have not really an opportunity of trying your horsemanship on any wilder steed than our sober Davy, or Old Hundred."

"For my part, I wish I had Pegasus here, at this moment," said the student. "I would mount him forthwith, and gallop about the country, within a circumference of a few miles, making literary calls on my brother-authors. Dr. Dewey would be within my reach, at the foot of Taconic. In Stockbridge, yonder, is Mr. James, conspicuous to all the world on his mountain-pile of history and romance. Longfellow, I believe, is not yet at the Ox-bow, else the winged horse would neigh at the sight of him. But, here in Lenox, I should find our most truthful novelist, who has made the scenery and life of Berkshire all her own. On the hither side of Pittsfield sits Herman Melville, shaping out the gigantic conception of his 'White Whale,' while the gigantic shape of Graylock looms upon him from his study-window. Another bound of my flying steed would bring me to the door of Holmes, whom I mention last, because Pegasus would certainly unseat me, the next minute, and claim the poet as his rider."

"Have we not an author for our next neighbor?" asked Primrose. "That silent man, who lives in the old red house, near Tanglewood Avenue, and whom we sometimes meet, with two children at his side, in the woods or at the lake. I think I have heard of his having written a poem, or a romance, or an arithmetic, or a school-history, or some other kind of a book."

"Hush, Primrose, hush!" exclaimed Eustace, in a thrilling whisper, and putting his finger on his lip. "Not a word about that man, even on a hill-top! If our babble were to reach his ears, and happen not to please him, he has but to fling a quire or two of paper into the stove, and you, Primrose, and I, and Periwinkle, Sweet Fern, Squash-Blossom, Blue Eye, Huckleberry, Clover, Cowslip, Plantain, Milkweed, Dandelion, and Buttercup,—yes, and wise Mr. Pringle, with his unfavorable criticisms on my legends, and poor Mrs. Pringle, too,—would all turn to smoke, and go whisking up the funnel! Our neighbor in the red house is a harmless sort of person enough, for aught I know, as concerns the rest of the world; but something whispers to me that he has a terrible power over ourselves, extending to nothing short of annihilation."

"And would Tanglewood turn to smoke, as well as we?" asked Periwinkle, quite appalled at the threatened destruction. "And what would become of Ben and Bruin?"

"Tanglewood would remain," replied the student, "looking just as it does now, but occupied by an entirely different family. And Ben and Bruin would be still alive, and would make themselves very comfortable with the bones from the dinner-table, without ever thinking of the good times which they and we have had together!"

"What nonsense you are talking!" exclaimed Primrose.

With idle chat of this kind, the party had already begun to descend the hill, and were now within the shadow of the woods.

Primrose gathered some mountain-laurel, the leaf of which, though of last year's growth, was still as verdant and elastic as if the frost and thaw had not alternately tried their force upon its texture. Of these twigs of laurel she twined a wreath, and took off the student's cap, in order to place it on his brow.

"Nobody else is likely to crown you for your stories," observed saucy Primrose, "so take this from me."

"Do not be too sure," answered Eustace, looking really like a youthful poet, with the laurel among his glossy curls, "that I shall not win other wreaths by these wonderful and admirable stories. I mean to spend all my leisure, during the rest of the vacation, and throughout the summer term at college, in writing them out for the press. Mr. J.T. Fields (with whom I became acquainted when he was in Berkshire, last summer, and who is a poet, as well as a publisher) will see their uncommon merit at a glance. He will get them illustrated, I hope, by Billings, and will bring them before the world under the very best of auspices, through the eminent house of Ticknor & Co. In about five months from this moment, I make no doubt of being reckoned among the lights of the age!"

"Poor boy!" said Primrose, half aside. "What a disappointment awaits him!"

Descending a little lower, Bruin began to bark, and was answered by the graver bow-wow of the respectable Ben. They soon saw the good old dog, keeping careful watch over Dandelion, Sweet Fern, Cowslip, and Squash-Blossom. These little people, quite recovered from their fatigue, had set about gathering checkerberries, and now came clambering to meet their playfellows. Thus reunited, the whole party went down through Luther Butler's orchard, and made the best of their way home to Tanglewood.

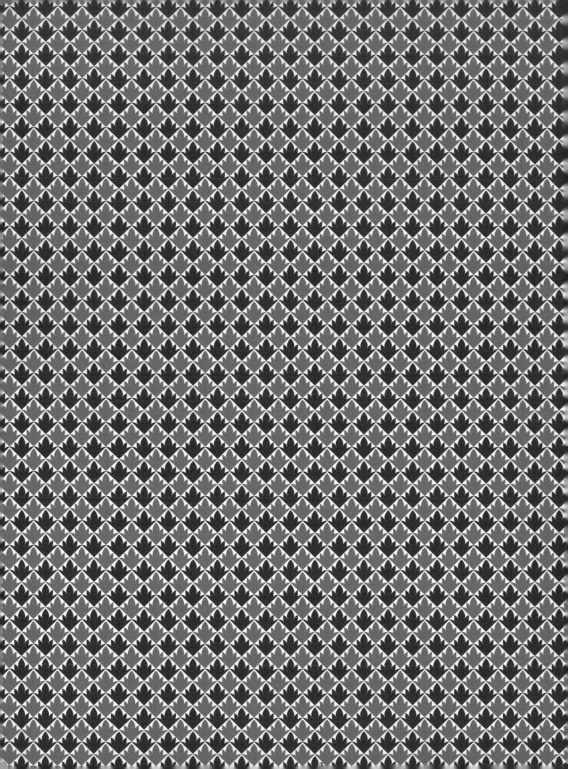